Does this
insecurity
make me
look **FAT?**

Does this *insecurity* make me look **FAT?**

MICHELLE WILSON

DESERET
BOOK

Salt Lake City, Utah

To my daughters, Paige and Grace
May they ever remember they are His daughters first

And to Grandma Jane, who believed in me before I did

Author's photo by Marianne Denney. Used by permission.

© 2013 Michelle Wilson

Library of Congress Cataloging-in-Publication Data
(CIP on file)
ISBN 978-1-60907-807-2

Printed in the United States of America
R. R. Donnelley, Crawfordsville, IN

10 9 8 7 6 5 4 3 2 1

contents

Contents

PART ONE

learn to see

Chapter One

all the little leaves

The Power of Perspective

What we think . . . determines who we are—
and who we will become.
Dieter F. Uchtdorf

Every day women are bombarded with temptations, demands, and decisions on the outside and troubled by unrealistic expectations, doubt, and fear on the inside. We are given the opportunity to choose what we will do, but all too often we second-guess those choices, allowing guilt, worry, and even shame to haunt us.

One of the many things I love about the gospel of Jesus Christ is how empowering it truly is. We know that with our God-given agency and through the miracle of the Atonement of Jesus Christ, we have the power to direct our own lives. A friend of mine shared a quote in church that encapsulates this idea perfectly. She said, "What is to be is up to me." We have the ability to overcome the bad and lay hold of the good. We have the right to decide who and what we will be, although it's not always easy to see things that way.

Now, if you are thinking that this book will be an extended pep talk, you are partly right. We all need a good pep talk once in a while.

In fact, the last chapter is titled "A Good Old-Fashioned Pep Talk," and you may refer to it for a quick pick-me-up when you feel down.

But this book is more than a pep talk. Like the Book of Mormon prophet, Nephi, my soul delights in plainness (2 Nephi 31:3). This book contains a plain and simple yet profound message: We can find joy, peace, and confidence when we learn to see ourselves, others, and life through God's eyes. Yes, there are some "rah rah!" and "you can do it!" elements sprinkled throughout this book. But it is really a call for women to stand up and be women and to shake off the false perceptions, insecurities, and doubts that hinder our happiness and keep us from fulfilling our divine responsibilities and potential.

We live in exciting times. Heavenly Father is directing a great work, and He needs us. He needs us to protect our families, to protect His standards, and to be a light in an ever-darkening world. He needs us to inspire and uplift, to edify and embrace those around us. We are more important than we know, stronger than we realize, and extraordinary in every way. He can see it, and I believe He wants us to see it, too. That's what this book is about.

Having laid that foundation, I will tell you about the most magnificent pity party I ever had.

Pity Party on Aisle Nine

Pity parties are like Twinkies: even though they're not good for us, sometimes we just can't help ourselves. Through the years, I've had my share of pity parties of all kinds—big and small, long and short. Some come unexpectedly, and some come like clockwork—such as those that come each spring when it's time to buy a new swimsuit. That's always a tough day.

My "maturing" body has become a larger, Picasso-esque version of what it was twenty years ago. The cruel morphing of time and age, coupled with the conspiracy of every clothing store to hang the most horrific fun-house mirrors in their dressing rooms, has fueled the nightmare that is swimsuit shopping.

The swimsuit-shopping pity party takes the same course every year: I go to four or five different stores and try on dozens of swimsuits. I curse the devil for inventing spandex, which cuts into my hips like a rubber band wrapped too tightly around a water balloon. I painstakingly pull each swimsuit on, grimace at what I see in the mirror—aging body and drumstick legs pouring over the seams of that devil-spandex—and then work up a glisten of sweat as I peel each one off. When I finish, the dressing room looks like a war zone, with swimsuit carcasses littering the floor. (I do clean up after myself, but, oh, how I wish I could just throw those suits down and stomp on them.) I leave empty-handed and heavy-hearted. Then I finish off my shopping day by eating large amounts of ice cream as I wallow in self-pity and try to figure out why gravity hates me so.

The beautiful thing about pity parties is that they are inclusive—they are open to anything that might be bothering you. What begins with mourning my long-gone pre-marriage figure segues into regrets about never learning to cook well and finishes with guilt for not reading to my freshly bathed children an hour every night as I lovingly tuck them into bed. At the start of my party I'm just fat, but by the end I'm a terrible mother, and I am sure my children would be better off being raised by Sister Homeschooling-Canning-Crafty Jones. It's exhausting.

It's a good thing my pity parties don't happen very often. It's also a good thing that I typically bounce back from them fairly quickly. Still, they happen more frequently than I would like. If it were up to me, I would place a permanent moratorium on all pity parties. Unfortunately, female nature, my propensity to expect too much from myself, and hormones don't allow that. Thankfully, the older I get (and wiser, I hope), the fewer and farther between they are. But they still come and go. In fact, it wasn't too long ago that I had a big pity party, the biggest I'd had in years. And it started out so small, because of a little piece of information that most people don't know about me—but which I am soon to reveal.

As a child, I lived what was, for all intents and purposes, a charmed life. Love was felt and the gospel was taught in my home. I was confident and carefree. I breezed through elementary school, getting good grades, singing in the choir, playing in the band, and carrying proudly the hard-earned title of "Cherry-Drop and Death-Drop Queen." (If you don't know what those are, find any woman who attended elementary school in the '70s—she'll explain it to you. If she is brave, she might even try to show you, but I wouldn't recommend it.)

My peak came at the end of sixth grade, when I graduated elementary school with straights A's. I sang a solo at the graduation ceremony. I was adorable up there onstage with my little dress and long hair and good grades. I was cute and smart, and I felt good.

Then summer came, and it all changed. My family moved to another part of town. I traded my long hair for a mullet (I still don't know why someone didn't stop me), and my face broke out in a full-force case of acne. To top it off, somehow my upper jaw grew that summer, giving me a gawky overbite. I started seventh grade friendless, self-conscious, and alone. I was relegated to the nerd category at my new school, and I found it hard to make friends at church.

It was the perfect storm of anything and everything that could go wrong, and my self-esteem plummeted, taking with it my hopes and goals for the future. I felt like a loser, and I acted accordingly.

Socially, I tried to keep a valiant front, but my formal education fell victim to misplaced priorities and crippling self-doubt. Although I was smart, I stopped performing that way. I treaded water through middle school, passing with B's and C's. High school was four years of feeling bad about myself and avoiding anyone, especially teachers, who showed the slightest degree of disappointment in me. And I gave them good reason to be disappointed. Many people avoid disappointment by achieving. I avoided it by avoiding classes. Each year my attendance, grades, and confidence dropped. By the end of my senior year, I found myself thirty credits shy of graduating.

Here comes that little tidbit that most people don't know about me: I didn't graduate with my high school class. In fact, I didn't graduate with any class. I didn't graduate high school, period. I never wore a cap and gown, never received a diploma. It was devastating and embarrassing, a failure of epic proportions. And yet I hid it with a smile and a blasé attitude as I signed up for classes at the local community college—only to fail there, too.

By the time I was nineteen, I was a high school dropout and carried a 1.0 college GPA. It was then that I finally took the GED (the General Educational Development tests that colleges accept in place of a diploma). That was the final nail in the coffin of my formal education—I told myself I was through with classes and tests. I was glad to be rid of them and tried to move on to "greener pastures," but I soon found that to be a difficult task.

I worked full-time at various jobs, spent time with friends, and dated. On the surface, I appeared happy—and I was, for the most part—but underneath, self-doubt, sadness, and fear festered. I had no direction and no long-term goals. And even if I had, I would have doubted my ability to achieve them.

When I was twenty years old, because of the counsel of my parents and my bishop and a sweet experience with personal revelation, I decided to serve a full-time mission for The Church of Jesus Christ of Latter-day Saints. This was a life- and perspective-changing experience for me. It was during this time of spiritual, emotional, physical, and intellectual preparation that I began to see and know God—and myself—more clearly. My joy and confidence blossomed as I found purpose and direction in my life and experienced success in my studies and teaching. I began to feel that I was intelligent and of worth. I began to feel like *me*, and I loved it.

It wasn't long after my mission that I met and married my husband, and our children soon arrived. My son was born when I was two months shy of turning twenty-five, and then a daughter came fifteen months later. As my confidence and perspective continued to change and grow during those early years of motherhood, I toyed with the idea of going back to school, but health issues and the needs of my young children kept the prospect at bay.

As the kids grew older, I tried a few times to brush away the academic dust. I took a class here and there as our schedule and finances permitted. Now that I was an adult, with maturity and a healthier perspective on my side, I did well. My confidence grew as I excelled in my classes, and I maintained a 3.83 GPA (which would have been a 4.0 if it weren't for that irksome muscle exam in my anatomy class).

In 2012, I again got the itch to return to school. I had done well in my most recent college classes, and I was feeling good. I decided to apply to a new college, and in order to do that I had to pull up all my old transcripts.

That was when the pity party kicked off.

I sat on my bed and looked at my high school transcript that screamed "Loser!" and then at my initial college stint, which also reeked of failure.

Good feelings gone.

I stared at the pile of papers in front of me. There, in official black and white, was proof that I had failed. The years of adult success, growth, and confidence were overshadowed by old high school feelings: *I'm not smart. I don't make good choices. I can't do this. I am going to fail.*

I was overwhelmed by negative emotions. And though the feelings did not fit with who I had become, they were very real and overpowering. It had been a long, long time since I had felt so down. I had to get up and walk away. I went into the bathroom and looked at myself in the mirror (because that's what they do in the movies, right?). A reflective analysis confirmed my doubts. Yep, I was stupid.

Now, you would think the awful feelings I allowed myself to feel would be sufficient fodder for a pity party, but that was just the beginning. While taking inventory of my educational and intellectual deficits, out of the corner of my eye I saw the bathroom scale jammed between the side of the cabinet and the bathtub, hidden away as a token of my firm resolution not to focus on weight but on being healthy. That week I had played tennis four times and had eaten healthy foods, and at that moment I needed a little good news. So I pulled the scale out and optimistically weighed myself.

I had gained five pounds. Good feelings gone again. Now I was stupid *and* fat.

I plopped down on the bed next to my pile of papers. That is when the first tear came.

My oldest daughter had a piano lesson that morning, however, and since a mother's work is never done, I wiped away my tears, put on my "brave mom" face, and drove her to her lesson. After I dropped her off, I did what any mature woman would do: I drove around, listened full blast to any sad song I could find on the radio, and cried while the list of my deficits that had started with "stupid" and "fat" grew. I was also a bad mother who didn't have any patience for her kids—not endlessly patient, like my friends were. I was selfish—not unselfish, like my friends were. I said weird things—not smart things, like many of my friends did.

I cried as I took inventory of all my apparent weaknesses, faults, and shortcomings. Then depression turned into dejection when I decided I was simply a worthless human being who was good for nothing.

I went on to spend the better part of that day feeling sorry for my stupid, fat self. I was impatient with my kids (of course, because I was a terrible mother) and not productive at all (because I was a terrible homemaker—not a good one, like my friends). No one wanted to be around me that day, and I didn't blame them because I was, of course, a worthless human being.

That afternoon, I decided to go to the public pool for exercise—because what makes a stupid, fat woman feel better about herself than squeezing into an old swimsuit at a public pool where the high school swim team happens to be practicing? My pasty hips bulged out of the bottom of my unforgiving elastic suit as I gasped for air while attempting the freestyle.

Free Willy.

Brilliant.

I topped off my day-long pity party by trying on clothes at the store. If I had been smarter, I would have known better. There's nothing like a dressing-room circus mirror to help me feel worse about my oversized pantry. (Note: "Pantry" is the nickname I have for my stomach, because it's where I store all my favorite foods.)

Needless to say, I looked terrible in every outfit I tried on. I left the torture room—I mean dressing room—empty-handed and as depressed as ever.

By that time, my pity party was in full swing. Self-pity, doubt, disdain, and regret were dancing with guilt, fear, and sorrow. They were having a heyday, and I was miserable.

The next stop was the grocery store. I walked through the candy aisle, cursing the two bags of M&Ms I had put into my basket. I'm pretty sure I heard the loudspeakers blare, "Pity party on aisle nine. Self-esteem and willpower spilled on the floor. Cleanup needed on aisle nine."

My evening didn't go any better. We had guests for dinner, and

I enjoyed their company, but it was difficult to be a great hostess (which of course I knew I wasn't—not like my friends, who had matching dinnerware and who used cute mason jars for cups). I was still feeling down, and I masked the pain with greasy food and sugary desserts (stocking up the pantry).

As I climbed into bed that night, the pity party was still going strong. I pulled out my journal and began to write. My pen flew as I wrote about mistakes I had made and opportunities I had missed. I wrote all about my regrets and remorse, my embarrassment and shame.

I still didn't feel any better. So I got on my knees and prayed. I prayed hard.

I asked God to help me: Help me feel better, help the pain go away, help me see myself through His eyes. I fell asleep on a pillow that was wet with tears. Then I woke up the next morning—and guess what? I felt better. How? My circumstances hadn't changed overnight, but my perspective had—and even that wasn't my doing. Heavenly Father did it.

I normally don't share such intimate thoughts about myself in this much detail—especially negative ones in a book that strangers will read. I share these feelings with you because I want to make it very clear that I felt bad—very bad. I want to make it very clear that *it was God who helped me feel better—so much better.*

He is the Giver of all that is good. He gave me peace. He gave me perspective. He gave me my smile back. He gave me *myself* back.

I also want to clarify something else that is very important. The devil is the *adversary* of all that is good. That is why I refer to him most often as "the adversary" in this book. He wants us to feel terrible about ourselves. I started my pity party alone—just me, my high school transcripts, and my thoughts. The adversary didn't start my pity party—I did. The more I focused on myself, the more I opened up my heart and mind to the adversary's influence. Somewhere along the way he happily joined in, cheering me on: "Yes, you are an awful person! No good, through and through." He pulled out his black pom-poms full of poison and waved them in my face while he sang, "U-G-L-Y! You ain't got no alibi! You're ugly! Yeah, yeah, you're ugly!" I started my pity party, and the adversary and I fueled it. Then God crashed my pity party, and for that I was grateful.

Rather than looking at where I had been and feeling bad for all that I hadn't done or all that I hadn't become, God allowed me to look at where I was at that moment and to see all the places I could go. I know I've made mistakes. I know I am not perfect. I know I'm not a size six—or eight or ten, for that matter. But I know that my Father in Heaven loves me the way I am.

My guess is that you've probably had days like that, where all your faults, weaknesses, disappointments, and misconceptions dog-pile on you and weigh you down. It's suffocating. You feel awful. You might be convinced that you are simply the worst person ever, and, if you're like me, you can probably come up with a laundry list of reasons to back it up.

But let me tell you: You are *not* the worst person ever. You aren't doing that poorly. In fact, you are probably doing just fine. If you don't believe me, ask God. If you feel down and out, pray to Him. If you feel lonely, desperate, depressed, or just plain terrible, seek Him out. Have faith. He is there. He will help. He may not change your circumstances (my pantry was still there when I woke up the next morning), but He has the power to help you change your perspective.

The spring after my grand pity party, I set off for my yearly swimsuit shopping spree, and, true to tradition, the swimsuits fell to the floor, as did my spirits. Half an hour into my first dressing room battle, my cell phone rang. It was my husband.

He said, "Hey, I just wanted to tell you how beautiful you are to me." He thanked me for bringing our children into the world, and he told me that he loves me just the way I am.

I turned, looked at myself in the mirror, and saw myself differently. I didn't compare my present self with my self of twenty years before. I saw myself now, as my husband saw me. For the first time in a long, long time, I stood in front of a mirror in a swimsuit and felt beautiful.

That is the power of perspective.

As I began writing this chapter, I pulled out my high school transcripts once again. They still looked the same—those terrible grades in black and white—but this time I saw them differently. I saw in them a lesson to be shared, not an indictment of my perceived potential (or lack thereof). I not only saw the grades differently this time, but I felt different. Despite the scattered showers of F's that dot the paper, I could look at them and still feel intelligent and capable.

That is the power of perspective.

If we could see ourselves, just for a moment, as God sees us, I am quite sure we would see beauty and magnificence that we never imagined. Our potential is amazing. Our future is brilliant. Our path is glorious.

You may have heard the saying, "God don't make no junk." It's true. God, our Father in Heaven, made me, and He made you—and we are not junk. He has told us that it is His work and His glory to bring about the immortality and eternal life of His sons and His daughters (Moses 1:39). Does that sound as though He views us as mistakes or that He is embarrassed by us?

Our Father knows us better than we know ourselves. He will never look down on us in shock and disappointment and say, "I didn't see that coming." He knows we aren't perfect. He knows we struggle. And He knows how great we really are. He knows what we can be and what He *expects* us to be. The key to our happiness—and our sanity—is to go to Him and let Him tell us what He sees in us . . .

and *believe* Him. It will change how we see ourselves, and in that change there is power, discovery, confidence, joy, and freedom.

How can perspective have that much power? Let me illustrate.

All the Little Leaves

When I was fourteen, my mom took me to see an optometrist, and I received my first pair of prescription glasses. They had large, clear, pink frames with pink-tinted lenses—highly fashionable in the mid-'80s. I loved how I looked in my new glasses: smarter, older, and obviously much cooler.

As my mother drove me home, I began to realize that not only did *I* look different in my new glasses but the world around me looked different, too. I could now read the once-blurry letters on the street signs, see the features on the faces of people walking down the street, even read the letters and numbers of license plates on the cars in front of us. Details were richer now, sharper and more defined. I could see the world around me more clearly.

As we drove home, I had a realization. I had seen these things a certain way my whole life, and now I understood that those things actually looked very different.

The most notable example was the big oak tree by the road that ran alongside my home. I had seen that tree a hundred times—it stood tall and wide, soft and green. However, that day, looking through my large, pink glasses, it looked different. It was no longer a fuzzy, soft green ball of tree but a giant, intricate cornucopia of leaves and branches. I could see the detail of each small limb, the outline of each delicate leaf. What was once a soft green mass was now an elaborate gallery of beautiful lines and shapes.

With my new glasses I could see the world around me clearly. Now I could see things as they really were.

Three weeks before I donned my new glasses—even the day before—I hadn't even realized I needed glasses. I just thought the world was how I saw it: soft and fuzzy. Until I was given the ability to see, I didn't realize how bad my vision was or how much I had been missing.

One of my favorite songs from the movie *The Prince of Egypt* tells about how wondrous life can be when it is viewed "through heaven's eyes." The song raises the question of whether a man can be judged by the things he builds or buys—and the reply is that you can't determine someone's worth through earthly eyes but only through heaven's, or God's, eyes (Schwartz, "Through Heaven's Eyes").

The world around me didn't all of a sudden change when I got my new glasses—but the way I saw it did. The tree had been the same for years, but to me it was different. Words appeared on the chalkboard at school where I had thought there were none. The clouds in the sky suddenly had defined shapes. The flowers in the field multiplied in number.

The miracle wasn't that the world had changed but that *my ability* to see it clearly had.

Many things may blur our spiritual vision of ourselves and the world around us. The way we view our lives can be affected by work, school, illness, stress, anger, frustration, jealousy, weakness, and countless other things. Because we all experience these challenges, we all see things from a polluted point of view.

Many people wear figurative "glasses" that offer different levels of clarity in the way they view life. Others aren't wearing any "glasses" at all—they simply walk through life in a state of spiritual nearsightedness, experiencing things in a "fuzzy" sort of way and missing the truths they would see if they focused on the important details.

Only God can see truth in its purest form—life as it really is, and us as we really are. Jacob taught this truth when he said, "O how great the holiness of our God! For he knoweth all things, and there is not anything save he knows it" (2 Nephi 9:20). God does know all, and He sees all in perfect clarity and truth. He has a perfect perspective.

How may we gain His perspective and see things through His eyes?

As we go to the Lord in prayer, our perspective can change. We can gain the ability to see glimpses of life through His eyes. These glimpses allow us to feel His love for us, His adoration for our children, His patience with others, and other miracles that we cannot always see for ourselves.

Perhaps even more important, as we go to Him, we will be able to see ourselves through His eyes. There is great value in that, especially for those of us who are haunted by the shadows of pity parties and their guests.

We can know who we were, who we are, and who we can become.

Afta Afta

In order to have the proper perspective, it's important to see how this life and the people in it fit into the grand scheme of things.

Somewhere between the heart and the mind there is a longing that is shared by people of all classes, races, religions, and nationalities. It's the inner petition of grown men and women and the hidden desire of rebellious teenagers, the longing to know who we really are. It asks the most humble and sincere questions: "Where did I come from?" "Who am I?" and "What is the purpose of life?"

In this world, there are those who believe our existence—everything we are made of—began when we were born into this life. They believe that our personality, our character, our preferences came to life at the same time we took our first breath. That school of thought preaches that there was a beginning point to our existence.

There are also those who believe that, since we had a beginning, we must have an end: the whole of our existence ends at death—we just cease to be. That reasoning begs the question: If the totality of our existence is encapsulated into this brief mortal life, then what is the purpose of it? If we have no ties to *before*, and no future *after*, how do we fit in *here*?

Heavenly Father knows our longing. I believe He gave us feelings of longing as a way to draw us back to Him, a way to lead us to the truth. In our darkest moments, when the minutiae of life no longer seem important, when we are stripped of pride and pretense, when we are in the throes of a massive pity party, we face our one intense desire: to know our purpose and our worth.

In my preteen years, *The Karate Kid* was one of my favorite movies. I bought all the issues of *Teen Beat* magazine that had Ralph Macchio on the cover. As an adult, I still enjoy the movie, but now I see it through different eyes. Nowadays Mr. Miagi fascinates me—there's something about a quiet, strong mentor who holds the secrets of life that I am drawn to.

At one point in the movie, Daniel, the young man befriended and tutored by Mr. Miagi, needed something. Unable to help him at that moment, Mr. Miagi responded in broken English, thick with a Japanese accent, "Afta."

Like many teenagers, Daniel was short on patience and foresight. Unhappy with Mr. Miagi's answer, Daniel asked, "After what?"

"Afta, afta" was his mentor's simple reply. No explanation, just "Afta, afta" (Kamen, *Karate Kid*).

For us, in the eternal sense there is an "afta afta"—and a *before* before. We know what comes "afta" this life—and even what comes after that—and we know what came before. We are not temporary beings. Each of us is an eternal being with a purpose that goes beyond the boundaries of this life. It has been said that we are not human beings having a spiritual experience but spiritual beings having a human experience (in Covey, *7 Habits*, 319).

We lived with God before we came here. The Lord Himself said to the prophet Jeremiah, "Before I formed thee in the belly I knew thee" (Jeremiah 1:5). He knew Jeremiah, just as He knows us, because we lived with Him before this life. The testimony of latter-day prophet Brigham Young confirms this truth:

"I want to tell you, each and every one of you, that you are well acquainted with God our Heavenly Father, . . . for there is not a soul of you but what has lived in his house and dwelt with him year after year; and yet you are seeking to become acquainted with him, when the fact is, you have merely forgotten what you did know" (*Discourses*, 50).

We lived with God before we came to this earth, and we will live with Him again. That is His plan for us. We don't remember our premortal lives—that forgetfulness is necessary so that we might live by faith. But as we learn about our true nature—the "before" and the "after"—we gain an understanding of the "now." With the help of our Father in Heaven, we can find nobility in ourselves, purpose in our pain, peace in our trials, and joy in the journey. As we find answers to that deeply planted longing to know who we are and where we came from, we find perspective and purpose. We find ourselves.

Sometimes the terms "God's perspective" and "eternal perspective" are used interchangeably. This makes sense, because God is eternal—as are we.

When we see with His perspective, the eternal perspective, life begins to make sense. We can see the beauty in places we hadn't seen it before. We can see problems as opportunities to learn, weaknesses as strengths yet to be developed, families as a forever unit.

That is the power that true perspective gives us. It opens the shades and floods our world with the light of understanding. In that light, we can see ourselves as He does.

We are beautiful, and we have a purpose.

When we begin to catch glimpses of who we really are, we can then begin to see the miracles that God can perform through us. There are people who need to be loved, to be served, to be taught, to be mended, to be healed. We are His hands here on earth, and our greatest joy is to be found when we are actively engaged in a good cause (D&C 58:27) and furthering His work and purposes.

I believe that there is a special purpose for each person's life. God has placed people in our paths that only we can help. He has provided us opportunities to learn and grow. But we can't hear His call to action if we are consumed with our worries, fears, and doubts.

This is our great quest: to change our perspective, to try to see life—and ourselves—through God's eyes. Only then can we begin to see our worth. Only then can we go to work lifting and building others—doing His work.

That is the great power of perspective. It is the lens through which we view ourselves and those around us, the lens that shapes our values, creates our opinions, and determines the direction of our footsteps. When we use the lens that God uses—when we see things through His eyes—we can see beyond our weaknesses and faults to the divinity that lies within us.

God's perspective allows us to see ourselves as eternal beings. We not only lived before we came, but we also fought valiantly for the opportunity to have a mortal existence. Using God's perspective, we can know why we are here and where we are going.

I wish that gaining the ability to see through God's eyes were as easy as donning a new pair of glasses. Unfortunately, it's not. It takes work. So let's get to it.

Chapter Two

does this insecurity make me look fat?
The Enemies of Perspective

*What you see and what you hear depends
a great deal on where you are standing.*
C. S. Lewis

Beginning with this chapter, I will capitalize the word *Perspective* when I am speaking about an eternal perspective, or the way God views things: in truth and light (D&C 93:36–37). Our path to gaining this Perspective is plagued by what I call the Enemies of Perspective: self-pity, fear, guilt, jealousy, doubt, and criticism, just to name a few. These enemies bind us to the false reality presented by the adversary, who wants us to be as miserable as he is (2 Nephi 2:27).

When my oldest daughter was fifteen, I shared an unspoken truth with her: every woman, young or old, has at one time or another felt she was the ugly duckling or that she was just not good enough. As women, we are sometimes plagued with unrealistic expectations and then burdened by guilt when we don't live up to those expectations. We allow fear of failure—or sometimes fear of success—to hold us back. We may feel unworthy, incompetent, and even unlovable. We compare our worst characteristics to someone else's best (remember how I did that during my pity party?) and feel we have fallen short.

These things are roadblocks to gaining that eternal Perspective. The key to overcoming them is honestly and sincerely recognizing that these Enemies are present in our lives and having the courage to let them go.

Pity for Sale:
Getting Rid of Things We Don't Need

A few years ago I held my very first garage sale—which is a big mistake for someone who tends to take things personally. Some people saw my things as treasures and took them home to enjoy. Others turned up their noses, leaving without purchasing a single item. Then there were the ones who never even got out of their cars. They slowed down just enough to get an idea of what I had to offer, and then, deeming it unworthy or undesirable, they just kept driving.

When it was over, I found myself with mixed feelings. I loved the extra money, but I hated the rejection. There is a part of me that didn't blame the people who didn't want my stuff. Some of the things I was willing to let go of were really great things, but I'll admit that some of the other things were not so great. In fact, as I went through things to set aside for the garage sale, I marveled that I had kept so much junk, some of it for well over a decade.

I wondered why I had held on to those things for so long. I hadn't needed them or even wanted them anymore. Still, they remained, shoved under my sink or hidden in a closet or at the back of a drawer. Some of them I had even forgotten I still had. Some of them I held on to for years because I wasn't ready to say good-bye (I'll miss you, old plastic ficus tree—sniff).

So why did I still have this junk? Why was it so hard for me to let go of it?

Not long after my garage sale, I was talking to a dear friend on the phone. She is a dear friend because I love her dearly, and I count our relationship a blessing. This friend and I had been close for many years. Then, a few years back, we had a "falling out." Over time, we patched things up, and now we adore each other once again. Although we live in different states, we keep in touch with visits and phone calls, sharing stories, laughs, advice, tears, and fears.

During this particular "catch-up" phone call, the conversation turned to our falling out. We realized that we had never actually discussed what had happened—we just kind of got over it. As we then shared what had happened from our own individual points of view, we were both surprised at the emotions that resurfaced—some of which were negative. We both had thought those feelings were long gone.

But the feelings were there, and had always been there, hiding in the backs of our minds, dormant for years. I found myself asking a familiar question, "Why do I still have this junk around? I don't need it anymore." I wondered why it was so hard for me to let go of things, including feelings. I knew I needed to do just that—let go. But how?

Then the garage sale came to mind. I pictured what it might be like if I could have an "emotional garage sale." I'd have a table with anger for $5, envy for $3, and offenses for $1. On the ground next to the table would be a basket of self-pity for free. Denial would be priced at $100—because I would be in denial of the fact that it is worthless. I'd even have my "issues" on hangers for $1 each and a bin of my fears marked "Make Offer." I would place all my undesirable feelings out for the taking.

I wouldn't, however, sell the love and the laughter—though I might share it with those who would actually stop and get out of their cars.

I realized that, even though an emotional garage sale was a fantastic idea, it probably wouldn't work. Even if it did, it wouldn't bring in much money. I mean, who wants someone else's problems when they already have their own? I realized I would have to get rid of those long-harbored feelings the old-fashioned way: *I had to let them go.*

Now, I don't recommend letting go of all residual emotions. As I said, I'd keep the joy and the laughter, the love and the adoration. But there were some feelings, such as doubt, guilt, and sadness, that I had held on to that were of no use to me. Those negative feelings added nothing to the relationship my dear friend and I shared. In fact, as our conversation delved deeper into the details of our falling out, the newly awakened emotions were unwelcome and distracting. They served no purpose other than to make me—and her—feel bad. I had to let them go.

How did I accomplish that? First, I recognized that I had those feelings and issues. Next, I understood the fact that I did not need them anymore. They did not apply to our relationship. They did not apply to who I had become. (They were as old as when "thongs" were what you called the things you wore on your feet.)

Then I made the choice to let them go.

It sounds like such a simple thing: just let go. If you've got a hot potato in your hand and it's burning you, you let it go. If you are holding a snake that's ready to strike, you let it go. If you are holding emotions that hurt, you let them go.

It is a simple notion—but not necessarily an easy one. That's where prayer comes in. I'm certain that God does not want us to harbor bad feelings. His plan is just the opposite. We exist that we might have joy (2 Nephi 2:25)! He didn't go to all of the effort of creating this great plan, this world, or providing for the sacrifice of His Son so that we could keep our pain and suffering upon ourselves and be miserable forever. We are meant to live our lives with joy and meaning.

Letting go is simple, but it can be a hard thing to do. To recognize and acknowledge what we are feeling takes work. We need to ask ourselves a few important questions and give some honest answers:

Do certain memories, people, or situations evoke negative emotions? If they do, we need to decide if those feelings serve any useful purpose. Do those feelings cause us to withdraw from the Lord? Do they cause us to feel less than we should be? Do they feed anger and resentment toward another person?

If our emotions and feelings cause us to move in a direction that is contrary to Heavenly Father's will, then we need to let them go. We need to give ourselves permission to forgive, to let go, to move on.

We should not let who we are now be compromised by who we were then. We are not the same person we were yesterday. With prayer and understanding, faith and forgiveness, we can be freed from old hurts and ill feelings. We can be purged of unneeded sadness, unnecessary anger, and unwanted pride. We can choose to be rid of negative feelings and make more room for forgiveness and joy and for peace and growth.

Sometimes the process of letting go is a bigger hurdle than we can handle alone. That's okay. Spouses, family, friends, Church leaders, and professional counselors can be wonderful resources from our Heavenly Father that help us eliminate roadblocks to our happiness and peace of mind.

Heavenly Father is on our side in our fight for Perspective. Our Savior is, too. The Atonement was accomplished as a way for us to be freed not only from sin but also from the burden of the sorrows and pains of this world. Jesus lovingly said, "Take my yoke upon you, . . . and ye shall find rest unto your souls" (Matthew 11:29). He suffered pain beyond comprehension so He could minister to us in *our* pain.

In this life we will not escape all pain. The great missionary Paul taught that "we must through much tribulation enter into the kingdom of God" (Acts 14:22). Experience with pain—for example, the remorse we feel during repentance—is necessary for our growth, but we will discuss that more later.

For now, let's take a closer look at some of the junk that we need to let go.

Sweet as Terror:
Our Need for the Approval of Others

A few years ago I was called to teach the CTR5 Primary class. At the beginning of class every Sunday I would give each child a few moments to share a piece of exciting news or an announcement. Inevitably, at least one of the five-year-olds in the class would announce they had just been to or were about to go to Disneyland—even though it usually wasn't true. They also would often give detailed accounts of injuries and bodily functions. Best of all were the funny stories they would tell about their parents—the kind of stories I know parents would not want their children to tell.

One Sunday, an adorable little blond curly-haired boy announced that "when we were driving down the street, we saw some guys riding motorcycles. They were doing tricks, so my dad called the police."

Another Sunday, at the end of a lesson on keeping the Sabbath day holy, I asked the children to think of something they could do when they got home to show Heavenly Father they loved Him. One of them named reading the scriptures. Another named praying. Then a sweet girl with wide eyes and long blonde hair said, "I'm going to watch Sponge Bob b'cause my dad says that Sponge Bob is the best thing ever and he watches it every day. Even sometimes when I am in bed."

I will refrain from immortalizing some of their other revelations in print. Suffice it to say that children have an overabundance of energy and a severe lack of discretion. They will tell you if they think you're fat or mean or your cooking is bad.

I once stopped a young boy who was barreling down the hallway at church. I leaned over and sweetly said, "Now, honey, you shouldn't run in church." He looked at me and said, "Your breath stinks" and then sprinted off toward the foyer. I straightened up to see three other adults within earshot staring at me. With flushed cheeks, I pointed to my mouth. "It's the cinnamon gum."

Out of the mouths of babes. You gotta love 'em—but I don't trust 'em.

Because of this experience, as a young mom I was nervous about the stories my children might tell. What if they told their teachers that I ate ice cream for lunch? Or that I ran a red light that one time? Or, heaven forbid, what if they told someone I wasn't a good mother? What would their teachers think of me?

I tried to coach them on what was appropriate to share in public and what wasn't. We were all doing just great—until the Mother's Day Tea.

On the Friday before Mother's Day at my children's elementary school, the first grade class held a Mother's Day Tea. My oldest daughter invited me to her classroom for juice and cookies, where she and the other students would take turns reading poems they had written about their mothers.

The mothers beamed as their well-groomed children read verses about flowers and hugs, puppies and laughter. I smiled wide as my daughter stood up to read hers. She looked like a little angel. She shuffled her feet, took a deep breath, and smiled sweetly as she began to read her poem:

> *Mom.*
> *Kind Mom.*
> *Loving kind Mom.*
> *Cool kind loving,*
> *Sweet, cool, kind, loving Mom.*
> *I love Mom.*

I sat there with a proud smile. Kids don't lie. See? I was a good mom.

My adorable daughter came and sat down on my lap. She smiled again as she asked if I wanted to read the other poems she had written in her book. I was so pleased with the first one that I could hardly wait to see what other brilliant words she had penned about me.

My smile faded as I read another one of her poems:

Mom

Is as sweet as terror.
Is as clever like a fox.
Is as strong as an ox.
Is as pretty as a horse.
Mom

Um . . . what was that?

My daughter beamed with pride. "One more, Mom," she said. I wasn't very excited about the one I'd just read, but there was no way I could have prepared myself for this masterpiece:

My Mom

My mom spanks me a lot.
My mom is mad a lot of times.
My mom is torture.
My mom.

I was horrified!

I looked up at my daughter, who was grinning from ear to ear. What could she be thinking? I mean, I may have spanked my children a time or two, but I had done nothing that would warrant this. Yes, I was a little irritable at times, but I didn't think I had an anger issue.

My cheeks warm, I looked around the room at the other mothers.

They were still smiling at their sweet, innocent little angels who had written so many wonderful things about them. I looked back at the demon-child on my lap. *Traitor,* I thought.

Out of the corner of my eye I saw the teacher walking toward me with her hand over her mouth.

"I—I have no idea where this came from," I stammered.

"I know." The teacher lowered her hand, revealing a grin. "If it were any other parent, I would have called the police, but I know you well enough to know that it's not true."

Relief replaced horror, but it was soon overtaken by anger. I turned to my daughter. "What on earth were you thinking?"

Still wearing a sweet smile, she said, "Mom, I thought it would be funny."

I'll show you funny, I thought. No ice cream for lunch tomorrow. Who will be laughing then?

The teacher's smile turned into a laugh. "You should be grateful the poems stayed in the book," she said. "She wanted to read all three of them in class, but . . . I thought that probably wouldn't be the best idea."

"Thank you for that," I replied wholeheartedly.

I turned back to the beast—I mean my daughter—who, for some mysterious reason, was still smiling. I raised my eyebrows (Mom-code for "This is gonna get real") and said, "Well?"

She threw her arms around me. "Mom, I love you. You're not totally torture. I just wanted to be funny—like you."

Ah. Combating impending retribution with compliments—sneaky, but effective.

I hugged her back, unable to stay angry. She was so cute, and, yes, she was really funny—but I was everlastingly grateful that the teacher hadn't let her read the other two poems in class. I might have died. I was also grateful that the teacher had the ability to look beyond my daughter's slanderous (albeit humorous, well-written, and completely false) statements. She knew the poems didn't define me because she knew the kind of person I was.

I like to think that perhaps God sees me that way. When I make mistakes, I like to think He says, "It looks like you really messed up, but I know you, and I know that isn't you." He knows my mistakes don't define me; they are an opportunity for me to change. He knows my shortcomings aren't permanent; they are opportunities for me to grow.

Still, there was a little part of me that worried what the teacher thought. What if she did think I was a bad mother? What if I was?

I shouldn't have allowed myself to ruin a sweet moment with my daughter because I was worried about what someone else might think. But it's easy to do, isn't it? We women do it a lot. We care about what other people think about us.

Is that a sin? No, but it can be damaging when we allow it to cloud our perception of who we really are. The scriptures say, "For as [a man] thinketh in his heart, so is he" (Proverbs 23:7). The way we think of ourselves is the rudder that determines how we treat ourselves. If we allow the opinions of others to govern our thoughts, then we are, in effect, allowing their opinions to govern our lives. That is a lot of power to give to people who are also imperfect.

A famous actress once said, "It took me a long time to learn not to judge myself through someone else's eyes." It is not easy to let go of what other people think about us, but it can be done.

A coworker once told me she didn't like me. She and I were very different. She was serious and pragmatic; I smiled and laughed a lot. She wasn't "touchy-feely"; I loved talking about feelings and lifting people up. She wanted to focus on work; I wanted to focus on people. It wasn't a matter of bad versus good—we were just very different.

One day, she told me, "I just don't get you, and I actually don't like you that much."

How do you respond to that? I smiled at her and said, "Well, I do. So it's okay." And it was true. I did like me, and I still do. Even if she didn't.

It wasn't easy for me to get to that point. In the first chapter of this book I told about my high school experience and my failure therein. In those days, there wasn't anything I dreaded more than the disapproval of other people, and there wasn't anything I longed for more than their approval. I wanted the teachers to think I was smart. I wanted the boys to think I was pretty. I wanted the girls to like me. I wanted my parents to be proud of me.

All of these desires weren't bad, but for me it went beyond having them see me a certain way. The way they felt about me became how I felt about myself. If a teacher gave me a certain "look," I felt stupid. If a boy said I was ugly—and this happened more than once—I was sure I was ugly. If my friends told me I was a bad person, then it must be true.

I sold my identity for the compliments and criticism of others.

I did not belong to *me*. I allowed *them* to tell me who I was and what I was worth. We do that sometimes. We seek the approval of our peers, our spouses, our bosses, our coworkers, even our own children. We want them to view us as being intelligent, giving, beautiful, worthwhile, talented, and so forth.

One problem with putting so much stock in the opinions of other people is that everyone has a different opinion. If you allow the opinions or approval of others to define your worth, you will continually ride a roller coaster of emotions from elation to despair and back again—even though you remain the same person inside.

With her permission, I share an experience my sweet daughter recently had. She was fifteen—the age when teenage girls are discovering who they are—and a boy she liked professed his feelings for her at a church dance. She told me with wide, gleaming eyes that he said she was "perfect." And she believed him.

Just two days later, this same daughter was told by a peer that she was "needy" and "not the same old girl we used to love." Through tears this time, my brokenhearted daughter told me how terrible she felt. In a matter of two days, she went from feeling perfect to feeling inadequate—and yet she was the same girl.

I sat with her and walked her through the two experiences. The light of understanding came into her eyes as she began to see what she had allowed these people to do to her feelings—for better and for worse. She saw that she had looked to them to tell her who she was and what she was worth.

When I asked to what source she should look to find her true worth, she smiled through moist eyes and said, pointing up, "Heavenly Father."

"And what does Heavenly Father think of you?"

"He thinks I'm pretty awesome."

And she believed Him. I hope she always will.

It wasn't until I was almost twenty years old, as I was preparing for my mission, that I had begun to understand the lesson I tried to teach my daughter that day. The more I studied the gospel and developed a relationship with my Father in Heaven, the more I knew I wanted to serve Him and love Him. As I began to learn how He felt about me, the opinions of other people didn't matter as much. I knew what He thought about me—and I believed Him.

I'm still not perfect in this area. There is a part of me that likes to be liked, of course. But no matter how bad I feel, I know *God* can see beyond my self-doubts and insecurities and fears. It doesn't matter if others don't understand me or even like me. They don't know me like God does. He sees all of me, He knows who I am, and He loves me.

I love knowing that! In my darkest moments, when I feel self-pity or despair, greed or selfishness, fear or pain, God can look beyond all of that and *see me*, and I know He thinks I'm all right. No, He thinks I'm amazing.

That's the power of Perspective. The opinion of another person does not define you. It merely shows *their* view of you. It reflects *their* reality, not God's.

Stephen R. Covey said, "The way we see the problem *is* the problem" (*7 Habits*, 40). In that same light, I'd like to propose that the way we see ourselves is the solution. If doubting yourself and seeking validation or approval from others is a big part of your life, please consider looking to another, higher, external source for the definition of your worth.

Only Heavenly Father can tell you your true worth—because it was He who created you. He can tell you how important you are, how special you are. You can hear Him and believe Him—and you can be confident.

Cool Beans: Comparing Ourselves to Others

Comparing ourselves to others is similar to seeking approval from others—but it's different enough, and prevalent enough among women, that it warrants its own section.

I drive a minivan. At first, I was like some people who swear they will never drive one. Then, after hauling a bunch of kids (okay, it was only two, but there were days when two felt like twenty) in a sea of California drivers for six years, I broke down and bought a red minivan. I loved it. I sat higher above the road, it had fantastic cargo space, and my children were out of hitting range from each other.

Oh, how I loved my red van.

Then one day I was rear-ended, and the van was totaled. My husband and I went to the dealership to buy another minivan.

The salesman pointed us to a van that had just come in. I loved the inside. It had a nice, gray, plush interior, a built-in DVD player, and captain's chairs in the middle row. But if the truth be told, I was not a fan of the outside. The maroon paint job wasn't too bad, but it seemed that every car I had owned since I was married had been either maroon or red, and I was ready for a change. The real turnoff for me, though, was the awful blue pinstripes that were painted across the sides of the van.

They were almost a deal breaker.

I swallowed my pride and bought the van, thinking that, if nothing else, it would keep me humble. It's hard to drive around feeling like "cool beans" in a maroon minivan with blue pinstripes. But over the years I have grown used to the color and the stripes. They actually come in handy when I can't remember where I parked. It's the only one with stripes like that. Seriously—the *only* one.

When it was time to take the van into the shop for its 90,000-mile checkup, the service people found a long list of things that needed to be fixed. They offered me a rental car while they worked on my van.

I thought I was going to get an old loaner vehicle, but they paid for a nice rental car—a Dodge Charger, black, with tinted windows.

Toward the end of my thirty-minute drive home, I pulled up next to another minivan at an intersection. It was an older model and it did not look awesome—not like my car or me. I was in a black Charger with tinted windows. It was official: I was cool beans.

Then I caught myself in mid-thought and had to laugh. Just an hour earlier, I had been rocking a minivan that was even uglier than the one next to me, and now here I was feeling like I was more awesome than the driver next to me because I was in a Charger—and it wasn't even mine!

I share this story to illustrate a point: My coolness, in my own eyes, was established when I pulled up to someone I deemed to be not as cool as I was. I compared myself to someone else and based my feelings about myself—superficial though they were—on how I felt I measured up in comparison to her.

This is sort of the reverse of what was outlined earlier in this chapter. Rather than basing my worth on someone else's opinion, I was basing my opinion of how cool I was on how *I* compared *myself* to someone else.

My husband tells our children, "Never compare yourself to others because there is always someone dumber, and there is always someone smarter."

We know that, but we still do it. We compare ourselves to our friends, to supermodels in magazines, and to members of our family. We then attach a sense of worthiness to ourselves based on that comparison. My stoplight epiphany taught me that: I was the same person in my pinstriped van as I was in the Charger—until my Charger pulled up to a van that was ugly like mine. Then I felt cool. How silly that something so insignificant can do that to us.

I sometimes jokingly say I like to hang out with older women because it makes me feel younger, but there is some truth to it. I went to a baby shower for a friend of mine, and one of the younger women looked at me and said, "Michelle, since you're the oldest woman here, could you share some of your sage wisdom that you've gained in all your long years of parenting with us new, young, and energetic mothers?" No, she didn't say it exactly like that, but that's how I heard it—and I felt old. I am always the same person, but sometimes I allow myself to feel different depending on who I am with. I can go to an all-you-can eat restaurant with my brothers and eat with abandon, but when I go out to eat with a bunch of women who are size four and ten years younger than I am, I am guilty of sucking in my pantry until it aches as I try to remember my table manners and curse the fact that I "forgot" to work out that week.

I love the writings of the Apostle Paul. He taught, "For if a man think himself to be something, when he is nothing, he deceiveth himself" (Galatians 6:3). Depending on the situation, I can think of myself in a certain way when I am actually not that way at all. When I do that, I am deceiving myself.

No matter where we are or who we are standing next to, we are still the same person—only our surroundings have changed.

This is where the importance of Perspective enters in. We need to remind ourselves that when we stand before the Savior at the final judgment, we will not be standing next to our peers. We will face Him alone, and I don't think He will care what car we drove, how rich we were, what kind of highlights were in our hair, or how expensive our clothes were. He won't ask how we compared to our friends or neighbors. He will want to know how close we are to being like Him.

He may ask what we did to serve Him. Did we apply the Atonement in our lives? Did we love and cherish our families, putting their needs before our own? Did we raise up our children in truth? Did we serve selflessly and love our neighbors? Did we magnify our callings? Did we contribute to our community? Did we keep ourselves clean and pure? Did we, indeed, receive His image in our countenance (Alma 5:19)?

He may not be as concerned about where our heart lies compared to our neighbors as where it lies compared to where it could and should be.

Thankfully, I know where my heart lies. I know who I am on the inside. I may falter occasionally, like I did at that intersection, but it usually takes me just a moment to bring myself back to the truth.

I may have an ugly van, crazy hair, a messy house, and imperfect habits, but I am trying to be like Jesus every day. And that is more than cool.

I encourage you not to worry too much about how you look compared to someone else. Remember, there will always be women who are larger or smaller, smarter or not as smart, cleaner or messier, a better or worse cook, and so forth.

It's not how you look when you stand beside a neighbor that matters. It's how you look when you face the Savior or when you kneel before your Father in Heaven to pray, all by yourself.

Paul teaches us: "Be not conformed to this world: but be ye transformed by the renewing of your mind, that ye may prove what is that good, and acceptable, and perfect, will of God" (Romans 12:2).

What is the will of God for you? He wants you to understand who you are, what you're worth, and what you can do.

When you understand that, you can be confident.

A Bear Is Going to Eat Me: Fear

Fear is another emotion—or state of mind—that stands in the way of having a true Perspective.

Allow me to share with you my experience of the last time I slept in a tent.

It was a cool, autumn night in Mount Rainier National Park. The walls of my tent were engulfed in the heavy darkness of the forest. I peeked out from my sleeping bag, moving nothing but one eye as I tried to see something—anything—that looked familiar and safe. What little air I shallowly breathed in was cold and wet, an assault to my senses.

Everything was dark—dark and still.

Though I saw nothing and heard nothing, I knew "It" was out

there—a bear—just waiting for the perfect time to grab a midnight Michelle snack.

Snap! The breaking of a twig confirmed my greatest fear. It was here.

I lay frozen on my back, preparing for what would happen next. My heart pounded so loudly I was sure the sound of it had led It here. I did not move, because I knew if I did, it would be the end of me. So I lay there, still, for what seemed like hours, listening to every sound that came from outside my tent. My mind raced with every grue-some scenario. Finally, and mercifully, fatigue set in, and I somehow drifted off to sleep.

I woke up the next morning to a tent full of light and with a grateful heart that I could live yet another day. It had not come to eat me.

Dramatic? Absolutely. I have—I'm working on "had"—this fear that while I am camping with my family, I will be eaten by a bear. Bears live in the woods. We camp in the woods. And so . . . I've seen this kind of thing happen on television—and you can believe every-thing you see on TV, right? It is inevitable, and I am terrified. Bears are scary, so to me what I felt that night was a perfectly logical and acceptable fear.

Unfortunately, this same fear that hijacked my night also affected my experience during the day. It prevented me, for example, from hiking with my family on that rarely used trail (where I knew the bear would be waiting). I couldn't enjoy s'mores or sitting around the campfire because I was sure the smell and sound would attract a hungry bear.

I loved to camp, but the fear of the Michelle-eating bear perme-ated every part of my experience. I couldn't fully enjoy what or who was around me. I allowed this fear to dictate my level of comfort, my level of activity, and my level of commitment. I allowed fear to control me. And I haven't slept in a tent since.

I confess this fear because it illustrates an essential yet often ignored eternal principle: Fear is bad.

Some people may argue that fear keeps us safe—hasn't mine kept me "safe" from the bear all these years? I will tell you that this argument doesn't hold water. Although fear does keep us from making certain choices that could lead to undesirable results, it can also rob us of opportunity, peace, and a fullness of joy in this life.

There's an old story of a farmer who was sitting on his steps chewing a piece of straw. A passerby asked him how the cotton crop was going that year.

The farmer replied, "There won't be any. I didn't plant cotton because I was afraid of the boll weevil."

"Well," said the passerby, "how's your corn?"

"Won't have corn, either. I was afraid there wouldn't be enough rain for the corn to mature."

"You must have planted potatoes," said the man as he looked out across the field of dirt.

"Nope. I didn't dare plant those, for fear of too many insects."

"So what did you plant?" the man asked.

"Nothing!" replied the farmer. "I'm playing it safe. Better to be safe than sorry."

I am convinced that Heavenly Father did not intend that fear be our rudder in life. I ask myself how many camping trips were ruined because of my fear. You might ask yourself a different question. How many new friendships were not nurtured due to fear of rejection? How many relationships have failed due to fear of commitment? How many experiences have been missed for fear of failure? How many apologies were not offered for fear of losing pride? How many prayers were not said because of fear they would not be answered? How many times have we turned down opportunities out of fear, telling ourselves we were "playing it safe," only to end up with nothing?

Paul taught, "For God hath not given us the spirit of fear; but of power, and of love; and of a sound mind" (2 Timothy 1:7). We should not let fear control us, but neither should we throw all caution—or a clear understanding of risk—to the wind. Perhaps that is part of what Paul meant by "power" and "a sound mind." God has given us intelligence and agency. These two things allow us to make discerning choices for ourselves.

We are endowed from on high with power to direct our lives, and, thankfully, we are not solely dependent on our own intellect. We can receive help, as Jesus Christ promised: "Peace I leave with you, my peace I give unto you: not as the world giveth, give I unto you. Let not your heart be troubled, neither let it be afraid" (John 14:27). Can you feel in these words the love and concern He has for us? Moroni taught that "perfect love casteth out all fear" (Moroni 8:16). It is through the love of our Heavenly Father and our Savior, coupled with our decision to trust Them and love Them in return, that we can begin to conquer our fears.

Perspective can give us the courage we need to hope, dream, and do. In the Book of Mormon we find the story of a woman named Abish, who acted with this kind of courage. Abish served as an attendant to the queen of a godless people. The king was known to be a harsh man. It was common for him to put to death those who disappointed him (Alma 17:28). Perhaps because of this, Abish, a long-time convert of the Lord, held her testimony inside—until one remarkable day.

Through circumstances that were miraculous in and of themselves, the king and queen experienced a spiritual manifestation so intense that they fell to the ground. Other servants cried in fear, but Abish knew they were seeing the power of the God she loved. She saw this event as an opportunity for the people she loved to become converted, too. Driven by newfound courage that was fueled by love and hope, Abish ran from house to house, telling all who would listen about what had happened (Alma 19:17). The king and queen awakened and testified of the Lord to the crowd who had gathered, and "as many as did believe were baptized" (Alma 19:35). Abish's courage led to the establishment of the Church among the Lamanites and commenced a great work among Abish's people (Alma 19:36).

We all fear something, but with the help of our Heavenly Father and our Savior, we can overcome our fears. The doors of opportunity will open to us, and we can live life as it is meant to be lived—with power, love, peace, and a full measure of joy. We can be confident.

The Rottenness of the Bones: Envy

Do you ever look at someone else's life with a twinge of envy? Perhaps it's that woman at church whose children look perfect or your crafty friend whose house is never messy or your thin friend who can eat anything she likes and never gains weight. Do you sometimes wish you could do what they do or have what they have? I've certainly done that.

On the surface, wanting something someone else has may seem harmless. In reality, however, envy is quite dangerous. Yoda, the fictional yet wise Jedi master, said, "Envy leads to jealousy, jealousy leads to hate, hate leads to anger, anger leads to the dark side" (Brackett and Kasdan, *Empire Strikes Back*). Envy doesn't seem too bad until you realize it's the first step toward becoming like Darth Vader!

A divine source tells us that "a sound heart is the life of the flesh: but envy the rottenness of the bones" (Proverbs 14:30).

What starts as an innocent longing or desire, if left unchecked, can unlock the doors to jealousy, greed, anger, and resentment. These negative emotions seep into the way we view others and what they have. *They don't deserve that nice car. She doesn't deserve that compliment. He doesn't deserve such an easy life. They don't deserve all that money.* Suddenly we become authorities on what others should be allotted—as if we have God's power and perspective to know what they truly deserve.

Envy can also be a canker on how we see ourselves and what we have. *Mrs. Jones is thin, so that means I am fat. My neighbor's house is bigger and newer, so mine isn't as nice as I thought it was.* We measure ourselves and our lives against theirs and allow the brightness of their talents, strengths, and successes to diminish our own. We allow envy to ruin our attitude—and our gratitude.

Of course, if we are continually envious of others, we will never see our lives, and even our selves, as good enough. This is the way envy gets in the way of our Perspective. How can we truly see and appreciate what we have when our sights are always focused on what others have that we lack? We can't.

If I were to ask you what the opposite of envy is, what would you say? Put the book aside for a moment and think about it.

What did you come up with?

My thesaurus offers "goodwill" as an antonym. I could add "kindness" and "love." Perhaps the word that fits best is "charity."

When we have charity toward others, we are truly glad when they prosper. We rejoice in their successes with no thought of comparing those successes to our own. We love other people, we serve them, and we are happy for them. Our view of them is not tied to our view of ourselves, and we allow them to simply be themselves.

The same thing applies to having charity for ourselves. We rejoice in our own successes, with no thought of comparing them to the successes of others. We love ourselves, we are good to ourselves, and we are happy with ourselves. Our view of ourselves is not tied to our view of others, and we allow ourselves to simply be who we are.

When with God's help we free ourselves from envy, we see ourselves and our lives through His eyes. We find joy in our trials, hope in our weaknesses, and excitement in our challenges. When we change our focus to Him and away from "them," we can love ourselves and others the way He wants us to—and we can be confident.

Help Thou Mine Unbelief: Doubt

One night I was working on an important writing project that was proving to be a challenge. I had prayed about it, and an undeniable answer had come, telling me that everything would work out. But even though Heavenly Father had answered my prayer, and I knew I would be supported and sustained in the good thing I was doing, the project wasn't going as I had planned. The words weren't coming easily, and when they did, I doubted them and my ability.

So I did what every mature woman does when she gets frustrated: I pushed my laptop back and pouted.

That lasted only a few moments. Then I prayed again.

It was the same plea the struggling father uttered in Mark 9:24: "Lord, I believe; help thou mine unbelief."

My eyes were drawn to the scriptures on my desk, and I felt compelled to pick them up. I fanned the pages with my thumb and opened the book randomly.

My eyes fell on the words of Paul: "Be of good cheer: for I believe God, that it shall be even as it was told me" (Acts 27:25).

I smiled and felt peace. It was a gentle, loving reprimand—a reminder that I, like Paul, should believe God will give me what He has promised, even if I might not be able to see it at the moment.

One of my favorite quotations from C. S. Lewis says, "Faith . . . is the art of holding on to things your reason has once accepted, in spite of your changing moods" (*Mere Christianity*, 109).

I had once accepted the answer I received, but when the struggle came, I doubted. I needed to have stronger faith in the Lord and the answer He had given me.

The Spirit touched my heart and filled me with renewed hope and motivation. It also filled me with a determination not to let myself waver again but to put my complete faith and trust in God.

This episode was a small hiccup in the big scheme of things, but it was a giant lesson for me that was two-fold:

1. Answers can be found in the scriptures, especially when Heavenly Father speaks to us directly through them.
2. I should not doubt God. He will deliver all that He has promised and more.

He would keep His promise to help me. My job was to have faith and write—and to leave the doubts behind.

This was fairly easy to do with a writing assignment, even as important as this one was. However, in our daily lives, doubt can be a heavy deterrent to our peace and productivity. We might doubt ourselves in any or all of the following areas:

• Abilities
• Decisions
• Hearing answers to our prayers
• Intelligence
• Talents
• Choices
• Parenting skills
• Thoughts
• Intentions
• Worth

To sum it up, we doubt ourselves.

Doubt creeps into our minds almost imperceptibly, attaches itself, and creates a canker of negativity and sadness. It stifles creativity, crushes opportunity, blocks answers from heaven, and chases away peace. That's a lot of damage for one little word.

As much as we know doubt is undesirable, getting rid of it can be a scary thing. The opposite of doubt is certainty. In a world of everchanging discovery and values, where one day we are told, for example, that eggs are good for us and the next day we are told they're not, we may become conditioned not to believe things with any degree of certainty. Why should we believe something when the next day it might change? We become accustomed to questioning and doubting.

In a world that is in constant flux, some doubts can be healthy. However, you will notice that the things in the list above are not worldly things. They are things that involve our inner world.

Through personal success, prayer, trust, and faith, we can learn to dispel the doubts in our lives. Mormon implored that we "doubt not, but be believing" (Mormon 9:27). Believe in what? Believe in God. Believe in His ability to help us, to make us equal to our tasks. With His help, we can believe in ourselves—and we can be confident.

Guilt Schmilt: Guilt

During a phone call, a dear friend and I exchanged personal updates and anecdotes about our lives. She was a very busy woman, with more responsibilities than I have purses (and that's a lot). The reason for this call was a confession of guilt on her part. I had asked her a few weeks before to do something for me, and I simply hadn't had the time to do it. She said she had felt too guilty to let it go. Of course I told her not to worry about it, but I could hear the heaviness in her voice. She was still holding on to the guilt.

We women can be awfully hard on ourselves. Even if we did overcome all of the other Enemies of Perspective, we would probably still find something to feel guilty about.

The complexity of our feminine nature produces some contradictory attitudes. We understand that a person should not feel guilty for inescapable imperfections, and we believe this is true for everyone we know and love—except ourselves. We are quick to pacify our friends' feelings of guilt by giving them familiar but heartfelt pep talks with sentiments such as, "You are doing the best you can." Yet when our attention turns to our own challenges, any feelings of tenderness, understanding, or acceptance go right out the window. We might as well be Mrs. Peacock in the study, holding the sullied candlestick. We are G-U-I-L-T-Y.

So is personal guilt beneficial in any way? Should we get rid of it? Can we?

To begin with, it's important to recognize that guilt may have two possible origins: cognitive and emotional—or, in other words, the mind and the heart. When the mind recognizes we have violated some standard, we logically know we have done something wrong. Many of these kinds of violations can be remedied simply by taking action or making some kind of effort. A parking ticket can be paid; a missed appointment can be rescheduled.

The other, far more complicated, origin for guilt is emotional. Emotional feelings of guilt often come when we don't live up to the expectations we have set for ourselves: We didn't speak as kindly as we should have. We didn't love as unconditionally as we should have. We didn't clean the house as well as we should have. We didn't raise our children like we knew we should have. You get the picture.

A guilty conscience often ambushes us when we fall short of our own self-imposed standards—and maybe especially when we fall short of the standards that we know God has set for us. Logic takes a backseat here. We are convinced that leniency, compassion, and forgiveness somehow do not apply to us.

Guilt isn't a one-trick pony. It may come as a small, almost imperceptible whisper—a twinge that fades in moments—or it may be a lasting but quiet uneasiness or a nagging feeling that gnaws at our insides. All across the spectrum, from an uncomfortable feeling to a paralyzing force that shuts down happiness and hope, we can be plagued by guilt.

Nor is guilt a loner. It has a large, active family, with relatives such as remorse, pain, regret, fear, and anger to cheer it on.

Can feelings of guilt be beneficial? On both the cognitive and the emotional levels, guilt can be constructive *if* it moves us toward positive action and emotion. In teaching the Corinthians about repentance, Paul wrote: "I rejoice, not that ye were made sorry, but that ye sorrowed to repentance. . . . For godly sorrow worketh repentance to salvation" (2 Corinthians 7:10). When we feel guilty about a transgression or an infraction of God's law, and it leads us to make things right, we feel better about ourselves. We might call this good guilt.

Guilt that moves us toward negative action, including no action at all, or negative feelings, such as inadequacy and unworthiness, is not useful. This is bad guilt.

We need to remember that usually it's not the standards that are the problem—it is how we feel when we don't measure up to them that trips us up. After all, it was the Lord who commanded us to be kind and loving and to raise up our children in righteousness (D&C 68:25–28). And of course we know intrinsically that a clean house is better than a messy house. But to always expect perfection from ourselves or to expect perfection *now*—or to expect to be as perfect as others look in circumstances other than our own—is unrealistic. We may gain comfort—and Perspective—from the words of former Relief Society general president Barbara B. Smith. She said, "Ideals are stars to steer by; they are not a stick to beat ourselves with" ("A Conversation," 8).

Below is a simplified equation of how bad guilt is created. It's as easy as A+B=C.

(A) Unrealistic expectations
+ (B) Misguided view of our performance and abilities
= (C) A guilty conscience

In order to eliminate a guilty conscience, we must have the opposite factors in our equation.

(A) Realistic expectations
+ (B) Honest and forgiving view of our performance and abilities
= (C) A healthy conscience

We must have realistic expectations of ourselves and an honest and forgiving view of our attempts and abilities. Is this easy to do? Not always. But the formula is simple and achievable.

For example, as I write this chapter, I am sitting with my laptop on my unmade bed, surrounded by three piles of laundry: one to be folded, one to be washed, and one that was folded until the cat decided it would make the perfect bed. Three boxes that had been sitting by my file cabinet are "waiting" to be put away, and a box of crackers from yesterday's snack is still on my desk. A few years ago I would have looked at this mess and felt guilty. I should have a spotless house, shouldn't I? What kind of a person leaves crackers from the day before on the desk? What a failure!

But today I don't feel that way. It took me a while to get from there to here. I have worked hard to have realistic expectations, and I have come to accept that, in all honesty, I am not always a tidy person. That doesn't mean I don't try to be tidy. It means that I try to see my messes for what they are: tasks to finish, not an indication that I am a failure or that I have a character flaw. This realization does not free me from the responsibility of keeping things orderly, but it has freed me from unrealistic expectations and unhealthy guilt.

Bad or unhealthy guilt weighs you down. Getting rid of it is quite liberating—like peeling off a drenched overcoat or unloading a backpack filled with bricks.

How do you become free of unhealthy guilt?

First, ask your Heavenly Father to help you honestly evaluate the expectations you put on yourself. Are they realistic? Is perfection expected today? Do you really need to bake and intricately decorate four dozen cupcakes for your four-year-old's birthday party? Are you a terrible person if you have a muffin-top? Must you save the *whole* world? (There is, of course, only one Savior.)

Second, again with Heavenly Father's help, lovingly readjust your expectations and give yourself a break! No one will be able to put a check mark in every box. We are not required to be all things, but we are asked to do our best. We are to magnify who we are, not necessarily what we do. An immaculate house, perfectly behaved children, and an unbroken record of punctuality will not matter if our character is tainted with pride, anger, selfishness . . . and guilt.

The laundry doesn't cry when it doesn't get folded. Neither should you.

Guilt is a thief that steals our peace, our confidence, our hope, and our ability to see things as they truly are. Guilt is an Enemy of Perspective.

Let it go.

Replace guilt with self-acceptance, self-love, and self-forgiveness. Only then will you be free to see yourself through Heavenly Father's eyes and to see the amazing person you truly are.

Don't feel guilty about it. Just let it go.

Let it go—and you can be confident.

Shame on You: Shame

Just as seeking the approval of others is similar to comparing ourselves to others, guilt is similar to shame. I think that shame may be the most damaging of all of the Enemies of Perspective.

Just as there can be healthy and unhealthy guilt, there can also be healthy and unhealthy shame. When we purposefully and knowingly act against the will of God, we may feel a strong sense of guilt, embarrassment, disgrace, or unworthiness—in other words, shame. If it fosters the desire to rid ourselves of these feelings through repenting, then it is good or healthy shame—shame that leads to good actions. We know we have acted poorly and have offended God and we are moved to make things right with Him again.

Bad or unhealthy shame is just the opposite. It includes feelings of guilt, embarrassment, disgrace, or unworthiness about who we are, not just about the sin we have committed. We feel shame for being a woman, for not being a better mother, wife, sister, or friend. This kind of shame is a weapon the adversary uses to keep us from God.

Think about a time when you felt ashamed of who you thought you were. Did you feel like praying? Did you feel worthy to pray? Mostly likely your answer to both of those questions is "No" because you felt distance between yourself and God.

Unhealthy shame, if left unchecked, can lead to severe feelings of hopelessness and even an abhorrence of ourselves. We can lose our Perspective and forget *who* created us and *why*. We can deem ourselves unworthy of love and pull away from those who desire to show love to us. We might even feel that we are unworthy of redemption, and we may turn our backs on God.

I have seen people who are suffocated by shame. Their eyes are hollow. Their hearts are hopeless. To see their empty smiles is heartbreaking.

For most of us, our burden of shame may not run that deep—but it can still be dangerous. When we feel ashamed of who we are or think we have little to offer, we may hold ourselves back from the people and opportunities that God has placed in our paths.

Satan knows this, and he finds great pleasure in seeing our struggles. The main goal of his sad life is to make us as miserable as he is. He knows that the ultimate misery is to be without God's influence and away from His presence. So he tries to take us there.

Shame is an awful self-disqualifier. It makes us want to hide from God's presence. But, in reality, when we feel shame is when we most need God and the power of the Atonement of Jesus Christ.

Some might argue that the opposite of shame is pride or honor. I'd like to submit that the opposite of shame is humility. We are not given weakness to bring us shame; the Lord gave us weakness to draw us to Him in humility. "I give unto men weakness," He said, "that they may be humble; . . . for if they humble themselves before me, and have faith in me, then will I make weak things strong unto them" (Ether 12:27). When you have humility, you understand your place in the world and your place before God. Humility is understanding the goodness—and greatness—of God and having the desire to become acquiescent to His will and His love.

When you are humble, you are able to see your weaknesses through His eyes. You see them for what they are: undeveloped strengths. You are willing to give away your sins to know Him (Alma 22:18), and you look forward to the day that you can be with Him again.

Peter admonishes us: "Humble yourselves therefore under the mighty hand of God, that he may exalt you in due time" (1 Peter 5:6). God's plan for us is that we be exalted, but we are not ready for that yet. Perhaps that's why Peter said that it would happen "in due time." God knows we make mistakes. He knows we are not perfect, and I'm convinced that He is not ashamed of us. So why should we be ashamed of ourselves? We shouldn't.

Let go of shame. See yourself the way God sees you: as His beautiful daughter. Allow yourself to be imperfect. Find hope in your imperfections, knowing that through Him they can be made strengths. Find peace in your weakness, knowing that through Jesus Christ you can be forgiven. Find joy in yourself—and be confident.

I chose the title of this book for two reasons: One, it makes me laugh. Second, and more important, it shows the power Perspective has within us.

When we look at ourselves through the lenses of the Enemies of Perspective—allowing others to define us, comparing ourselves to others, and giving in to fear, envy, doubt, guilt, or shame—we can become insecure in who we think we are. We may see ourselves as fat, stupid, unworthy, incompetent, or a plethora of other things that simply are not true to our eternal identity.

We must remember that these are tools of the adversary to keep us from experiencing joy, reaching our potential, and assisting God in His purposes. Paul exhorts us never to "give place to the devil" (Ephesians 4:27)—or to succumb to his tools and tactics that thwart our perspective and purpose.

When we begin to combat these Enemies, we begin to see ourselves as our Father does—not as who *we* think we are, but as we truly *are*. We can feel beautiful. We can feel worthy. We can feel that we are ready to be tools in His hands—and we can be confident.

Chapter Three

i'm right here

Understanding Our Relationship with God

Every time we reach out, however feebly, for Him, we discover
He has been anxiously trying to reach us.
Jeffrey R. Holland

Our self-confidence relies on our Perspective, which comes, in part, from the way we perceive how God feels about us. In that light, to make sure our Perspective is as accurate as it can be, let's spend some time getting to know God better. This chapter is broken into three sections:

Who God is.

How He sees us.

What He expects of us.

Only when we have a true understanding of our relationship with God can we see ourselves as we truly are.

Who Is God?

My son has always been a climber. At first, his conquests were couches and chairs. When he was three, he graduated to playground structures, small trees, and even doors. At that time, his favorite movie was *The Princess Bride*. He loved the hero, Westley, who seemed to have the ability to overcome any obstacle, even the tallest of cliffs, which in the story were accurately called The Cliffs of Insanity.

My son wanted to emulate Westley's climbing prowess. I tied several knots in a sheet and hung it on the inside of our front door. With a floor of soft pillows beneath him and a black bandanna like Westley's around his head, he would scale to the top of the door, proclaiming, "Look, Mommy, I'm Westley. I'm climbing The Cliffs of 'Sanity.'"

As my son grew bigger, so did the things he would climb: large trees, rock walls, railings—anything he could pull himself up and over.

One afternoon, after his fifth grade class had been dismissed, my son climbed up a railing at his school, then turned to jump over it. His feet didn't clear the railing, and he toppled over headfirst, about six feet to the gravel below. Instinctively, he held out his hands to break his fall.

I rushed him to the emergency room. I could tell he was in a lot of pain and was afraid of what would happen to him at the hospital, but he kept his head high and didn't cry.

After two hours of x-rays and waiting, the verdict was in. When his arms broke his fall, the fall also broke his arm. And even though his arms had helped to cushion the fall, he hit his head on the ground hard enough to cause a big bump—and an even bigger concern. The doctors ordered an MRI to check for further damage.

It was the first time my son had ever experienced that type of test. He was led to a cold, white, sanitary room with a large horizontal tube in the center of it. Inside the tube was a table where my son would lie. I was by his side as my hurting boy climbed onto the uninviting table. The technician explained that the table would be inched into the darkened tube, where the scan would take place. During the test, my son would need to remain completely still to ensure the accuracy of the test results.

He looked at me with nervous eyes, and I smiled a reassuring smile. It was then that they told me I couldn't be by his side during the test. Due to the radiation, I had to move to the room next to him. It was hard for me to leave. I knew my child was afraid. I knew he was in pain, and I wanted to be right there holding his hand.

But I couldn't. He couldn't undergo the test if I were by his side. So I went into an adjoining room. I could see him through a window, but he couldn't see me.

He called, "Mom, are you there?"

"I'm right here," I assured him. "Are you all right?"

His response was sweet and so full of faith. "Mom, as long as I can hear you, I'll be okay."

"Son, I love you," I said. "You will be just fine."

I was able to talk to him throughout the procedure, and he was able to keep his head perfectly still so that no retakes were necessary. Thankfully, there was no concussion. We left the hospital a few hours later, with my son sporting a new cast on his broken arm and my arm hooked through his other one.

To this day, I am still touched by the love and faith he had in me—and that he still has. In return, my love for him reaches depths I had not known I could feel.

A friend of mine once said, "Mortality is the proving grounds for eternity." We are here not just to prove ourselves to God (Abraham 3:25), but to prove to ourselves what we are made of. This world is fraught with sadness, risk, and danger. We experience sorrow because of our own choices, because of the choices of others, and sometimes because of the choices God makes on our behalf. While we are here, we can sometimes feel very alone.

But two truths transcend any book, lesson, or religion: First, *God is our Father in Heaven.* Malachi reminded the wicked priests of his day, "Have we not all one father? hath not one God created us?" (Malachi 2:10). Jesus repeatedly referred to God as "Father," saying, "Call no man your father upon the earth: for one is your Father, which is in heaven" (Matthew 23:9). And Paul, as he stood on Mars' hill, echoed the poets' words when he declared, "For we are also his offspring" (Acts 17:28).

The second truth is this: *Our Heavenly Father is keenly aware of us, and He loves us beyond our comprehension.* I believe He aches when we ache and rejoices when we rejoice. All that He is and all that He has accomplished has been for us. If He thought it would be in our best interest, He would move heaven and earth to protect us from pain. But He knows that only through resistance do we gain spiritual strength. So, for our benefit, He stands behind the windows of heaven as we are tested.

Although we cannot remember Him or see Him, He is only a call away. When we look up to the heavens from the world where we feel alone and ask, "Father, are you there?" He looks down and says, "I am right here. I love you, and you'll be just fine."

He stays His hand to protect our right to make our own choices. That is how much He loves us.

I love my son. I could have run in there and climbed into that scary tube with him in an effort to comfort him during the test. I could have pushed the technician out of the way and taken my son home, freeing him from the frightening procedure. Heaven knows I considered doing both of those things, but that would have ruined the test. He had to go through it alone in order to find out what needed to be fixed and to get the help he needed.

There have been times in my life when I have asked God to come down and vanquish my enemies, to remove the tests that lay before me, to show Himself to me, to let me physically feel his paternal embrace so that I would know He is real—but He has withheld those things from me because He understands they would ruin the test. He understands that I need to go through this life—tests, trials, and all—in order to learn and grow. He knows that pure knowledge of Him at this time would trump my faith, and it is through my faith that I must prove myself in this life.

I have heard people say that if God loved them, He would spare them from their pain. What they do not understand is that He allows us to be tested *because* He loves us, *because* He knows what we can do and what we need to do, and *because* He sees us for who we really are: His children who have the divine right and innate ability to become like Him, their Father.

My son was not entirely alone during his test. I was just around the corner, as close as I could be, watching him and talking to him. We are not left completely alone, either. Our Father in Heaven is just around the corner, as close as He can be, watching us and communicating with us as we experience our tests in life.

How Does God See Us?

Because we know that God is our loving Father in Heaven, logic tells us that He looks upon us, His daughters, with the tender love of a parent. He loves us with charity, which is a perfect love. He sees beyond our performance to our potential, past our faults to our future, and through our doubts to our divine nature. He sees us as His daughters, His heirs, and His greatest creations.

A few years ago, I planted pumpkins in my garden for the first time. It was a warm summer, and the pumpkins grew large. It was a great harvest, and it brought our family great joy. This year I decided to plant pumpkins again. I opened the envelope of seeds and poured them into my hand, smiling at them with admiration. They were smooth and fairly large—but I wasn't admiring the size of the seeds. I was thinking of what the seeds would become. They were not just seeds in my hands—they were pumpkins-to-be. I was excited not because I held a handful of seeds but because in my small hand I held the promise of a garden of pumpkins that would bring us joy.

We are all like seeds. We come in different shapes and sizes with different colors and needs. We all have the same purpose: to grow into something more—much more—than a seed.

I am convinced that when God looks at us, He smiles not only because of who we are now but because of who He knows we can become. He sees the promise of our divine future, the lives we will touch, the weaknesses we will overcome, His work we will accomplish. I think He finds joy in the fact that we, as His children, have divine DNA to enable us to become like Him.

Because He sees all that we *can be* does not make Him think less of who we *are now*. Yes, we are imperfect. We mess up, but we really try hard, don't we? It seems that He doesn't dwell on the negative. When our sins are forgiven, they are forgotten. He assures us, "And their sins and iniquities will I remember no more" (Hebrews 10:17).

God looks not just at our performance but also at our hearts. He sees our hopes, our desires, our longing to do good and be good. He sees who we are on the inside. "For the Lord seeth not as a man seeth; for man looketh on the outward appearance, but the Lord looketh on the heart" (1 Samuel 16:7). "I the Lord search the heart," He tells us (Jeremiah 17:10).

We adopted our youngest daughter when she was six years old. With her traumatic past, it was understandable that she had some emotional and behavioral issues to overcome. As her mom, I felt it was my duty to immediately love her and embrace her. But, as hard as it is to admit, there were times when I found this to be a difficult task.

One day when I was really struggling, I received some wonderful advice that changed my perspective forever. I was told that children—all people, in fact—have two parts to them. The first, and the most visible, part consists of our actions or our behaviors. These are the things we do or don't do, say or don't say. The second part, which can be harder to see, is what is inside the person—our intentions, our hopes, our potential.

The problem is that sometimes our behaviors can be such a thick covering that it is difficult to see past them—like a mummy wrapped in cloth bands. That day, I was told that you do not have to love behaviors, but you love the person.

I rejoiced at that advice. It helped me to separate what my daughter *did* from who she *was* and *could be*. I set to work "unwrapping" what I saw, and as I did that, I realized I was growing in my ability to look past her wrapping and see glimpses of her heart. She was, and still is, beautiful, and she continues to amaze me with her faith, her growth, and her spirit.

God must have an amazing heavenly x-ray vision that gives Him the ability to look through our layers of poor behavior and choices to what is underneath—our hearts. This does not mean He excuses our poor choices, especially our sins, for we know that He cannot look upon sin with the least degree of allowance (D&C 45:16). However, I think He sees our sins and mistakes as separate from our eternal identity. They are a part of the wrapping that we spend our lives removing through continual repentance and growth to reveal our true selves. God looks through the things that can blind and bind us; He looks into our hearts. He sees who we are now, coupled with who we can become, and I believe we are beautiful to Him.

There is nothing God doesn't know about us. The scriptures are replete with verses about the omniscience of God. He sees all that we are, think, and do—good and bad. Yet He does not view us as evil creatures to be ashamed of or to be pitied.

We are His children. He looks upon us with love, compassion, mercy, and confident expectation that we can overcome whatever is in our path.

He sees us as unique, lovable, and valuable women, whom He trusts to aid in His great work.

He sees our strengths, talents, and gifts.

He sees our love for others and our desire to help them.

He sees our ability to sacrifice and give unselfishly.

He sees the great influence we have on the family and the world.

He sees our desire to love and serve Him.

He sees our desire to be wanted, needed, and loved.

He sees our yearning for growth and progression.

He sees our ability to do and succeed.

He sees where our treasures lie.

He sees our purpose and our role in His plan.

He sees our hearts.

And we bring Him joy.

He loves us not *in spite of* ourselves but *because* we are who we are—beautiful, powerful, and remarkable women.

It is hard not to feel good about yourself when you read that list.

It is imperative that we understand how God sees us because our self-perception plays a vital role in our happiness and our ability to be tools in His hands. When we are bogged down by the Enemies of Perspective and allow them, rather than God, to define who we are, we thwart our ability to accomplish the things He knows we can accomplish. Doubts and fears hold us back from believing in ourselves—or believing in Him.

When we understand *how* He sees us and *who* we are, we can begin to understand *what* He expects from us.

What Does God Expect from Us?

Years ago, I read in a child psychology class that children tend to live up to the expectations that are placed upon them. If you see your child as stupid and expect that she will never amount to anything, that expectation will seep into your words and actions—and the child will believe you. On the other hand, if you expect your child to do great things, that expectation will blossom from your words and actions—and the child will believe you.

As we grow older, not only are we influenced by the expectations of others but we also begin to develop our own expectations of ourselves and the world around us. We tend to live up to those expectations, and so does our world. If we expect—or fear—we might fail, most of the time we will not try or we may try half-heartedly and apologetically—and we fail. If we think the world is a cruel and unfair place, that is where our focus will be and we will surely find it to be so. If we expect to do well, chances are we will do well.

We see what we expect to see. We become what we expect to become.

This, then, brings up the question: What does my Heavenly Father expect of me?

You've heard of the Ten Commandments. Well, in answer to the question "What does Heavenly Father expect of me?" I offer what I call the Nine Expectations. The word *expectation*, in this sense, resides happily within its family of synonyms: hope, belief, probability, and potential. To "expect" means to hope, to imagine, to wish, to anticipate.

These Nine Expectations might also be called the Nine Hopes

or the Nine Wishes, but I chose *Expectations* for a reason: "hopes," "wishes," and "anticipations" rest on a foundation of *confidence*. Based on my study of the scriptures and my experience with personal revelation, these Nine Expectations are things that I believe our Father not only *hopes* we can do, but *knows* we can do. I believe He is confident that we can live up to His expectations, which are these:

God expects you to be imperfect but to hope and to strive continually for improvement.

God expects you to live optimistically, with obedience, hope, and faith.

God expects you to seek Him out and allow Him into your life.

God expects you to forgive yourself, to learn from your mistakes and weaknesses, not to condemn yourself because of them.

God expects you to be patient and kind with yourself.

God expects you to be His hands on earth, helping others, and allowing others to help you.

God expects you to seek knowledge.

God expects you to have joy.

God expects you to overcome and be triumphant.

These are things that God hopes for us, that He wants for us. These are things that He has *planned* for us. These are things that He knows we can achieve and obtain. Reread the list and realize these are things you can do, things He wants you to do, things He expects you to do. He has great faith in you. These Expectations are not only within your reach but within your rights as His heavenly child.

You'll notice that one of the greatest commandments God has given us—the commandment to love others—is not included in this list. I haven't included it here because it is such an innate part of who we are, such an intrinsic characteristic of our souls, our motives, our longing that I don't think we need to be told or reminded of it. We love—it's what we do as women. But we do need to be reminded now and then of the other things on the list.

Why does God expect so much of us? He expects much because He loves much. He expects much because He can see much—He can see everything, every part of us. He knows what we are capable of. He wants us to hear Him and believe Him. When we begin to understand what He expects of us, we will be amazed at how well we can, with His help, live up to those expectations. We will have a life that is more free of self-inflicted adversity and pain. We will have a stronger relationship with God, a greater love for ourselves, and a greater ability to tap into the strength and saving power of the Atonement.

Let's explore each one of the Nine Expectations.

Expectation 1: God expects you to be imperfect—
but to hope and to strive continually for improvement.

This might be my favorite one because I do the being imperfect part really well. Jesus said, "They that are whole have no need of the physician, but they that are sick" (Mark 2:17). If being beset with sins, weaknesses, and shortcomings were a physical illness, we would all be sick.

The Savior's words show that our imperfections are not a surprise to Him or to our Father in Heaven. They know we make mistakes, and that we will make them until the day we die. That is what this life is for: *to draw those imperfections out into the light so we can see them and take them to the Lord to be changed into perfection.* Elder Joseph B. Wirthlin testified of this beautiful truth: "Oh, it is wonderful to know that our Heavenly Father loves us—even with all our flaws! His love is such that even should we give up on ourselves, He never will" ("Great Commandment," 29). In this life we prove to ourselves who we are, what we can do, and what we can become.

Although we don't have much information about Philip, one of the original Twelve Apostles of Jesus Christ, we do know that he, like all of us, needed to progress in knowledge and understanding. In John 6 we find Jesus and His Apostles on a hillside, where thousands had gathered to hear the Master teach. Jesus was about to perform a miracle—creating food enough to feed five thousand people from five loaves of bread and two fish.

"When Jesus then lifted up his eyes, and saw a great company come unto him, he saith unto Philip, Whence shall we buy bread, that these may eat?" (John 6:5). Even though Jesus knew He was capable of feeding the masses, He took the opportunity to allow Philip to prove his faith: "And this he [Jesus] said *to prove him* [Philip]: for he himself knew what he would do" (John 6:6; emphasis added).

The latter part of this verse, of course, may mean that Jesus knew what he, Jesus, would do—that He would feed the masses through miraculous means. But it is very instructive to read it with the meaning that Jesus already knew what *Philip* would do.

The Lord knew that Philip would have a limited, earthly view of the situation: he would see that there was not enough food (John 6:7). Perhaps Jesus wanted Philip to be aware of that limited view so he could then recognize the contrast between his earthly perspective and the heavenly miracle that was about to unfold.

Philip's reaction to the miracle is not recorded, but during the Last Supper he had another opportunity to learn to look beyond his mortal view.

In John 14, we read that Jesus taught His Apostles that "no man cometh unto the Father, but by me" (John 14:6). And then He said, "If ye had known me, ye should have known my Father also: and from henceforth ye know him, and have seen him" (John 14:7).

Philip replied, "Lord, shew us the Father, and it sufficeth us" (John 14:8). Philip's faith had grown—he believed that Jesus had the power to show them the Father. But he still did not understand what Jesus had meant when He said to the Jews, "I and my Father are one" (John 10:30): Jesus and His Father are so completely united in purpose and mission that to see one of Them is to also see the other. Jesus responded, "Have I been so long time with you, and yet hast thou not known me, Philip? he that hath seen me hath seen the Father; and how sayest thou then, Shew us the Father?" (John 14:9). Jesus went on to teach Philip and the other Apostles to "Believe that I am in the Father, and the Father in me" (John 14:10, 11).

Philip's understanding was not perfect. He still had more to learn, but he was moving in the right direction. I call this the Eternal Trajectory. How far along we are on the path may not be as important as the fact that we are headed in the right direction.

Another thing we need to remember: Philip's faith and understanding may have been imperfect, but *Jesus chose him to be His special witness*. In fact, it seems that Jesus sought him out at the beginning of His ministry: "The day following [Peter's call to follow Jesus] Jesus would go forth into Galilee, and findeth Philip, and saith unto him, Follow me" (John 1:43). Jesus called Philip, knowing the level of his faith and also knowing the growth that Philip was capable of.

Heavenly Father and Jesus Christ know we are imperfect. Still, they call us to action because they know what we are capable of. Elder Jeffrey R. Holland said, with a twinkle in his eye, "Except in the case of His only perfect Begotten Son, imperfect people are all God has ever had to work with. . . . He deals with it. So should we" ("Lord, I Believe," 94).

We are here to prove ourselves, to see with our own eyes, to hear with our own ears, to feel with our own hearts, to choose with our own agency. Our goal is perfection—*His* definition of perfection—but that goal will not be reached in this lifetime, and He knows that. Remember, we have been given imperfections and weakness to draw us to Him. We are the way we are now so that later we may become who we are to become. We are perfectly imperfect, and that's not only okay—that's His way.

Expectation 2: <u>God expects you live optimistically</u>, with obedience, hope, and faith.

Optimism is hope coupled with confidence in a successful outcome of something—whether it be a relationship, a business endeavor, a project, or a person. To live optimistically means you retain a hope and a confidence that your efforts will bring success, that good will come from bad things, and that you will come out on top.

We know that is true because the Savior Himself said, "Fear not, little flock; for it is your father's good pleasure to give you the kingdom" (Luke 12:32). He also promised the kingdom of heaven to those who are poor in spirit (Matthew 5:3) and those who are persecuted for His sake (Matthew 5:10). "Come, ye blessed of my Father," He said, "inherit the kingdom prepared for you from the foundation of the world" (Matthew 25:34). Those who follow Him will inherit the kingdom of heaven. That makes sense, doesn't it? As children of God, we shall inherit all that our Father has. We can have treasures in heaven that will never dim, glory that will never fade, and joy that will never die. Is that not something to look forward to?

To be a part of His "little flock," we must follow Him. "Keep my commandments," He pleads repeatedly in the scriptures, for He knows that obedience will bring us joy. "If a man love me, he will keep my words: and my Father will love him, and we will come unto him, and make our abode with him" (John 14:23).

This life is not our destination; it is merely a part of the journey. Granted, it is a difficult part—but it is only a part. I know that Heavenly Father and Jesus Christ want us to experience joy as we live in obedience to His will. There is more to life than our mortal eyes can see, and there is a kingdom waiting for us in heaven. When we keep our eyes focused on our destination—the kingdom of heaven—it helps give us the Perspective that feeds our optimism.

When our children were young, our family took a trip to Disneyland. We told the kids where we were going, showed them pictures, and shared our childhood memories of joy-filled trips there. Our children climbed into the car with great enthusiasm. They knew where they were going, and their excitement could not be contained . . . for about twenty minutes. Then one of them got hungry, and the other one had to go to the bathroom. Soon they were fighting or their rear ends were sore because of the car seats or they were bored or they were tired. The list of complaints went on.

"How much longer?" came the moans from the backseat. "Are we there yet?"

Even though I encouraged them to take heart and trust that the destination would be worth the trip, they soon lost all confidence that we would ever make it. They were irritable and whiny as they focused on the long drive rather than the destination.

It was a long day for all of us.

Years later, when our children were older, we made the trip again. This time things were different. The drive was the same, but the children's ability to understand and remain focused on the destination made the trip far more enjoyable. They knew where they were going, and they looked forward to their destination with confidence and great enthusiasm. There was hardly a complaint, and the drive was actually fun!

The travelers and the destination for these two trips were the same—what made the difference? Maturity and focus. The more mature my children were and the more they kept their destination in the front of their minds, the greater was their ability not only to accept the long ride but also to find joy in it, knowing where it would ultimately take them.

It is the same with us. This life is our path to an eternal destination. When we lose sight of where we are going and allow ourselves to wallow in the difficulties of the journey, we can become miserable. However, when we make an effort to grow and mature in the gospel and remain focused on that destination, our journey becomes filled with purpose and joy. Nephi eloquently captured this truth in these inspiring words: "Wherefore, ye must press forward with a steadfastness in Christ, having a perfect brightness of hope, and a love of God and of all men. Wherefore, if ye shall press forward, feasting upon the word of Christ, and endure to the end, behold, thus saith the Father: Ye shall have eternal life" (2 Nephi 31:20).

That is one of my favorite verses in all scripture because of the hope and peace it brings me. We look forward with a brightness of hope to the time when we will see our Father in Heaven again. We understand that in order to become like Him, we need to follow the commandments of His Son. We glory in the fact that, as His children, we have the right to call down divine help and guidance, comfort and strength on our journey. We are grateful that He has given us the beauties of the earth, our minds to think, agency to choose, relationships to hold dear, people to love, and the opportunity to be forgiven and to grow.

Our hearts fill with love for Him as we acknowledge His gifts to us, His love for us, and His plan for us. We eagerly seek out His will in our lives, trusting that He will never lead us astray. We feel safe in His arms. We feel whole in His love. We feel protected and guided on the journey back to Him.

His expectation is that we will make our journey with the optimism that Perspective affords, that we will live obedient to the commandments He has given us, and that we will hold fast to the faith we have in Him.

When we think about everything *He* has done, being joyful is not a hard thing for us to do.

Expectation 3: God expects you to
seek Him out and allow Him into your life.

My mother is a "bottom-line" woman. When she has a story to tell, it is short and to the point. I know she would love this concise verse from Paul: "Pray without ceasing" (1 Thessalonians 5:17). Like my mother, Paul got straight to the point: Pray. Don't stop. Ever.

I know that your Father in Heaven has things to tell you, favors to ask of you, gifts to give you—and many, if not most, of those things can be unlocked only through prayer.

Well-known author and preacher Max Lucado said, "People struggle with life when they don't have answers. The darkest valleys are blackened by the shadows of question marks. So what do you do? Think harder? Try harder? Hold longer conversations with yourself?

"Why not pray to the One with all the answers and let Him take over?" (*Max on Life*, 80).

God knows all the answers. He has the power to give us what we need when we need it. He has the desire and the ability to guide us through this life, sparing us unnecessary pain and sorrow, toward knowledge, growth, and joy. Who would not want that?

We want it, and so does He.

God will share His knowledge with us; He will give us the answers that we need. He speaks to us in many ways: through the inspiration of the Holy Ghost, through the words of others, and through the scriptures. I love the old saying, "If you want to talk to God, pray. If you want God to talk to you, read the scriptures." I've had many wonderful experiences while reading the scriptures that have solidified my testimony of this teaching. One particular experience is most precious to me.

One day I was in my room, and tears had been falling for almost an hour. I had been on my knees, praying for relief, for peace—for some acknowledgment that I was heard, that I was not alone. But none of those things had come.

I sat on my bed, feeling the weight of my problems pull my shoulders and heart down. I felt so alone. I glanced at my scriptures by my bedside. That old saying about wanting God to talk to you popped into my mind, so I picked up my Bible. In an act of faith and simple exhaustion, I closed my eyes and whispered to the heavens, "Please, tell me something." Then I let the book fall open.

I looked down at the page and read, "And when the Lord saw her, he had compassion on her, and said unto her, Weep not" (Luke 7:13).

Warmth from the Holy Ghost filled my heart and testified to me that that passage of scripture—those very words—were the words my Heavenly Father wanted to say to me. I was overwhelmed with a feeling of love and comfort. My Father in Heaven not only heard me but He spoke to me in a way that was unmistakable. He loved me, and He didn't want me to cry.

I did weep again, but this time I shed tears of gratitude and joy. I knew I was not alone. I knew that God had heard me, and I knew that I had heard Him.

Every experience with the scriptures may not be this momentous, but each one is an opportunity to reach out to our Heavenly Father and try to hear what He has to say.

He wants us to hear Him, and He wants us to allow Him to help us.

My youngest daughter has always been an über-helper. It doesn't matter what I am doing—making dinner, doing the dishes, painting my nails—she wants to be there, right by my side, helping.

One day I was making a seven-layer salad for Thanksgiving dinner. She wanted to do everything from chopping the celery (which

I didn't let her do) to licking the homemade dressing off the spoon in between stirs (I didn't let her do that, either). Then she wanted to help me clean up (which I did agree to). The day continued in this way as she followed me around, asking, "Mom, can I help?"

I soon became less than enchanted with her enthusiasm, and I began telling her no. Still, she continued to ask. Finally, she looked up at me, with her hands on her hips, and said, "Mother, why don't you just let me help you?"

The question was born out of sheer frustration on her part. She wanted to help, and the only thing standing in her way was my unwillingness to allow her to do it. My reluctance had nothing to do with whether or not I *needed* her help—I just didn't want it right then.

I think of my Heavenly Father and how often He wants to help me—and the only thing standing in the way of my receiving His offers of help is me. I imagine Him standing before me, watching me struggle, and saying, "Michelle, why won't you just let me help you?"

We so deeply want to be heard and to be helped, but when the help comes, we often turn it away. Sometimes we feel unworthy of His help. Sometimes we are prideful and don't want to be helped in His way. Other times we simply might not recognize His help.

But know this: When we pray to Him with faith and sincerity, God does answer our prayers. Jacob admonished, "And while His arm of mercy is extended towards you in the light of the day, harden not your hearts" (Jacob 6:5). It is up to us to hear Him and to accept His answers. It is up to us to *let Him help us.*

Satan will do all he can to prevent us from praying. Satan would have us feel we can't be heard. He wounds our spirits with lies that we are unworthy to be forgiven, unable to change. He whispers to us that our imperfections make us unlovable, that our mistakes ruin the lives of those we love.

Satan knows the great power we women hold in our families,

our congregations, our neighborhoods, and, yes, even the world. He knows that praying to our Father multiplies that power. If we let him, he will make us doubt our ability and worthiness to pray and then doubt the answers that we receive.

Here is the truth that the adversary works so hard to hide from us: *There never has been nor ever will be a time in our lives when God does not want to hear from us.* I know that He not only wants to hear from us but He longs for us to hear Him. He has a great work to do here on earth, and He calls for our minds, hearts, and hands to do the work. We need to let go of the Enemies of Perspective, seek out our Heavenly Father, and let Him into our lives. Sometimes we plead to be forgiven and yet, when He offers relief, we reject it on the grounds that we feel we don't deserve it. In doing that, we place our judgment above His. We seem to say that, even though *He* deems us worthy to be forgiven, we are not worthy—as if we know better than He does. But of course He knows all. And He wants us to pray to Him, even though, as the Savior said, "your Father knoweth what things ye have need of, before ye ask him" (Matthew 6:8).

My daughter still wants to help me with everything. I'll admit that most of the time it's easier to do things myself. But I have made a sincere effort to let her help me more. Last Christmas, for example, I was putting up Christmas decorations, and she asked if she could help. We worked together for about twenty minutes, putting up a garland and ornaments on the stairway banister. When we were finished, we stood back to admire our work.

She looked up at me and said, "Mom, thanks for letting me help you."

"Thanks for helping me," I smiled.

Then she hugged me. "I really love you," she said.

I looked down at her and realized that her desire to help me wasn't just because she liked to help. It was because she loved me. My heart melted.

Heavenly Father sends help to us not because He doubts our abilities but because He loves us and He wants to help us increase our abilities.

Seek Him out. Get to know Him. Learn to hear Him. Allow Him into your life. Let Him help—and let Him show His love for you.

Expectation 4: God expects you to forgive yourself,
to learn and grow from your mistakes and weaknesses,
not to condemn yourself because of them.

The vast topic of forgiveness warrants not just a chapter but an entire volume. For the purposes of this book, however, I wish to address this subject in terms of forgiving ourselves. This is difficult for many women to do. We tend to hold on to our mistakes like poisonous life preservers, unwilling to accept the peace that comes from being forgiven.

I am convinced that God expects us to forgive ourselves. Unresolved issues and pain can fester and boil under the surface of our lives. They can hinder our ability to love ourselves, to love others, or to feel loved. Punishing ourselves for past mistakes that He has forgiven us for is like paying a speeding ticket that has already been paid, insisting that even though the debt is clear, you still feel the need to suffer. It makes no sense.

The price for our sins has already been paid by Jesus Christ. Yes, we must repent and seek forgiveness for the wrongs we commit, but once that forgiveness is extended, *our acceptance of it is crucial.* If we do not accept His forgiveness—and forgive ourselves—we are not allowing the power of the Atonement to fully work in our lives. We are rejecting His help. We set ourselves apart, and we are alone. We view ourselves as broken and condemned, and that is simply not the case.

Many years ago I was given a beautiful candleholder as a gift. It had an antiqued, three-legged iron base that held a beautiful etched-glass bowl. It quickly became one of my favorite decorations and I displayed it in the most prominent places of my home.

One day as I was dusting, I dropped my beloved candleholder. Thankfully, the glass bowl didn't break, but upon further investigation I saw that one side of the iron base had been dented. The candleholder was now flawed. I wasn't ready to part with it, though, so I arranged it in such a way that the dent was hidden from view. But I still knew it was there. As time went by, I moved the candleholder from place to place, but I could never find a spot where its dent could not be seen. Eventually, I tucked it away in a cupboard in my bathroom.

One day I had the notion to clean out my bathroom cupboard. I sat down and pulled various discoveries from the cupboard abyss: cotton balls, an old watch, crusty nail polish, eight different half-empty (or half-full, if you're an optimist) old bottles of shampoo . . . and my old friend, the candleholder.

I looked sadly at its flaw, the dent in its base. Then, for the first time, I had the thought to try to smooth out the dent. I had never tried this before—the candleholder was made of iron, and I figured it was too strong to bend back. But this day I held the iron base in one hand, and I pushed out on the dent until my poor thumb turned white. Then—voila!—it worked! The dent was gone! I couldn't believe it. Years of banishment for my candleholder were remedied in five seconds of effort!

I placed the candleholder proudly on my bathroom sink where I could see it every day, and it is still there.

There are times when we treat ourselves the way I treated my poor candleholder. We look at our flaws—our weaknesses and mistakes—and feel they are too hard to fix. Perhaps our weakness or mistake has hurt someone else. Perhaps it has hurt us. So we tuck it away, embarrassed, ashamed, or maybe even hopeless about it, and surrender to the false notion that we can't be fixed. Or maybe we think we don't deserve to be fixed.

We look at our flaws as though they are evidence of our worthlessness and unworthiness. But that is simply not true. We are fixable, and we are most definitely forgivable.

Our weaknesses provide the opportunity—and the need—for us to seek out the One who can heal us. He told Paul, "My grace is sufficient for thee: for my strength is made perfect in weakness" (2 Corinthians 12:9), and the same is true for each of us. Through His Atonement, Jesus Christ has made it possible for our weakness to be made into strength. Our weaknesses are not our condemnation; they are our stepping-stones to Him.

To this the Apostle Paul said, "Most gladly therefore will I rather glory in my infirmities, that the power of Christ may rest upon me" (2 Corinthians 12:9). If anyone had reason to dwell on his mistakes, it would be Paul. His actions brought death upon many Christians, including the stoning of Stephen.

We know he felt anguish for his sins, his weaknesses, and his flaws. Perhaps this was part of the reason he did not eat or drink for three days after the Lord appeared to him on the road to Damascus. However, when he was forgiven and baptized, he *immediately* went forth and did the will of God (Acts 9:20). He spent no more time dwelling on his mistakes and weaknesses, except to give God the glory for strengthening him. He said, "I . . . glory in my infirmities, that the power of Christ may rest upon me . . . : for when I am weak, then am I strong" (2 Corinthians 12:9–10).

God has a great work to do in us and through us. He expects us to trust Him and to trade our weakness for His strength. He would like us to beat our spiritual plowshares into swords and our spiritual pruninghooks into spears, so that we may say, "I am strong" (Joel

3:10) and "fight the good fight of faith" and "lay hold on eternal life" (1 Timothy 6:12).

He expects us to make mistakes and then to learn from them. That takes humility. The Savior said that "he that shall humble himself shall be exalted" (Matthew 23:12). This is part of the plan. Our imperfections, our shortcomings, our faults, our weaknesses—they are all part of the plan.

He also expects us to accept His forgiveness and move on. Enos was a perfect example of this. He was reared in the learning of the Lord and yet he made his own share of mistakes. One day (about 2,500 years ago), Enos was hunting alone in the wilderness. It was then that the burden of his sins brought him to his knees. His soul hungered for forgiveness, hope, validation, and peace. He prayed all day and into the night. It appears that Enos was wracked with guilt.

At last, a voice came to him, saying, "Enos, thy sins are forgiven thee, and thou shalt be blessed" (Enos 1:5). Enos's response was powerful. In the next verse, we read, "And I, Enos, knew that God could not lie; wherefore, my guilt was swept away." What trust Enos had in God! The deep level of pain and guilt he felt had kept him on his knees for hours, and yet, in the moment that he felt God's forgiveness, Enos let the guilt go. Then, when he had let go of his personal guilt, he turned his focus and his heart to others.

Enos's ability to accept the Lord's forgiveness gave him the freedom to feel joy and peace. And when his heart and soul were no longer hampered by guilt, he was able to be a more effective tool in God's hands. For the rest of Enos's life, he taught and testified of Christ because His trust in God's forgiveness first allowed him to forgive himself. In the same way, our trust in God's forgiveness will allow us to forgive ourselves. When true repentance is sought, God does not hold grudges—and neither should we.

Our imperfections and sins should not be a stumbling block on our path to our Heavenly Father and our Savior. It is through recognizing our weaknesses and faults and our efforts to master them with Their help that we become like Them. That is a glorious endeavor, indeed.

Expectation 5: He expects you to be
patient and kind with yourself.

If you're anything like me, you have very high expectations of yourself. I know who and what I want to be, and when I don't live up to that, I can feel disappointed and even upset with myself. I should know better than to raise my voice when my child shoves clean clothes in the dirty-clothes basket because it's easier than putting them away. I should be less defensive when my teenager suddenly becomes an expert on how I should parent the younger children. I should remind them more kindly to wash their hands before they eat.

As we were growing up, my cousins would always say, "Life is full of 'shoulda dones.'" I know that I *should* do a lot of things that I don't do. In fact, I mess up a lot. I stay up too late, don't eat in a healthy enough way, am impatient, have unrealistic expectations, get annoyed with my kids and my husband, don't manage my time well, don't exercise enough . . . It's depressing to consider how long my personal list of things I think I need to improve could really be.

The Savior told his Apostles: "In your patience possess ye your souls" (Luke 21:19). We must be patient with our imperfections as we strive to improve ourselves. We will not become perfect overnight— most likely not even in this lifetime. Forty years from now, I will still be imperfect—hopefully greatly improved but still imperfect. So why beat myself up for something that is probably not attainable?

My older daughter loves to draw. A few years ago she told me she had decided she wasn't going to draw anymore. When I asked why, she said that no matter how hard she tried, she couldn't draw as well as her friend, and she was convinced she never would. So she gave up.

I took her to the store, and together we picked out a how-to-draw book, an artist's sketchbook, and pencils with big erasers. Now that she was equipped with the proper tools and helps, I encouraged her to continue working on her dream.

"Be patient with yourself," I said. "You will make mistakes, but that's what the erasers are for."

"But I don't want to make mistakes. I want to draw good *now*," she lamented.

"You will," I said. "That's part of the process. But you can't get better until you try and try and keep trying. It will take work, so be patient with yourself. Have fun with it. You'll get better—you'll see."

She was skeptical, but she took the supplies back to her room to reclaim her artistic pursuit. Now, years later, her talent has grown. She's gone through dozens of sketchbooks and hundreds of erasers, but her skill has improved, and she is a very good artist. More important, she has found great joy in pursuing her talent.

When we are patient with ourselves, we are able to more clearly see what is around us. It becomes easier to allow Heavenly Father to bless us. When we slow down and are patient, we become the tamer of our desires, the master of our emotions, and the possessor of our souls. We become free to see and to be.

As well as being patient, we must also be kind to ourselves. Heaven knows I have an alphabetized list of all the things I don't like about myself filed in the back of my brain. There are a lot of things I wish to change and a lot of things I am trying to improve. Sometimes I look at the things on that list in a very negative way. Not only can I be impatient with myself, but I can also be cruel to myself, like I was during that pity party, where I was convinced I was fat and stupid.

When my daughter comes to me and expresses negative feelings about herself, it breaks my heart. I know how bad she feels, how much she hurts. I want her to see in herself all the wonderful things that I see in her. I want her to know that the negative things—perceived or real—are only temporary, that with the Savior's Atonement and love, she can work through and past them. I want to hug her and make her pain go away.

That must be how Heavenly Father feels about me when I go to Him with my list of all the things I don't like about myself. I know it must make Him sad to see me punish myself so severely. He wants me to see the wonderful things that He sees in me. He wants me to know that my weaknesses and faults are temporary—that they are strengths in embryo. He wants me to know that the Savior's Atonement and love can help me work through and past my mistakes. I believe He wants to embrace me and make my pain go away.

I can tell my daughter over and over how I feel, but until she decides to see things differently, she will be miserable. I have the power to teach and reach out, but only she has the power to change herself.

It must be a similar situation between us and our Heavenly Father. He has the power to teach us and to reach us, but only *we* have the power to change our minds and our Perspective. That is so much easier when we treat ourselves with the patience and kindness He has for us.

Expectation 6: God expects you to be His hands on earth,
helping others and allowing others to help you.

I have a confession to make. Sometimes I find the messages in certain inspirational books to be a bit shallow. They seem to say that life is hard and all I have to do is believe and all my dreams will come true. But my soul longs for a deeper message. I think God expects more of us than to simply believe and dream.

Yes, life is hard. We don't need a book to tell us that. But it takes more than just believing to make any dream come true. It takes work. The scriptures tell us that God expects us to show our faith by our works. "By works a man is justified, and not by faith only" (James 2:24). God does not want his daughters to lie down in self-pity and despair, licking their wounds and focusing only on themselves.

I believe that the Lord desires us to stand up and be strong and courageous women, ready and willing to be His hands here on earth. One of my heroes, Eliza R. Snow, did not mince words when she said: "Women should be women and not babies that need petting and correction all the time. . . . We know the Lord has laid high responsibility upon us, and there is not a wish or desire that the Lord has implanted in our hearts in righteousness but will be realized, and the greatest good we can do to ourselves and each other is to refine and cultivate ourselves in everything that is good and ennobling to qualify us for those responsibilities" (*Minute Book*, 26–27).

I love the boldness of those words. (Something tells me Eliza would feel the same way I feel about those shallow inspirational books.) Eliza touched, or, rather, hit on an important truth: God has a great work to perform, and we have been called to participate in it. "And we know that all things work together for good to them that love God, to them who are the called according to his purpose" (Romans 8:28). We are called by Him for His purposes, great and small. He wants us to stand—imperfect yet perfectly willing—and heed His call.

Women don't usually need to be reminded or encouraged to help one another. We are drawn to the needy, we root for the underdog, and we care for the crying child. Often unbeknownst to us, we are God's answers to many people's prayers.

It is a struggle sometimes, though, for us to accept help from others. We may be drowning, and yet, when someone offers us a life jacket, we smile sweetly and say, "Oh, no, I've totally got this. I'm good"— while we are breathlessly sucking in air and water and our arms and legs are reaching the point of exhaustion. God often helps His children *through* His children, and I believe He expects us to accept that help.

My father taught me how to vacuum when I was a child: Straight lines. Always vacuum in straight lines, he told me. If vacuuming were an art, he would be the Michelangelo of suction. The Saturday morning routine in my home was to vacuum every room in the house. I always dreaded it, but we did it—and my dad made sure we did it well. We learned that part of loving something is taking care of it.

When my children were very young, I experienced some medical problems that caused me to often be "out of commission." It was a difficult time for our family, with a one-year-old and a two-year-old underfoot and my husband working two jobs. I struggled to meet my children's needs, let alone their wants. They wanted to go to the park, but I wasn't strong enough. They wanted to take walks, but I was in too much pain. I was tormented by guilt, fear, and sadness. I often prayed for comfort and relief.

One afternoon my dad called to check on me. It had been a particularly rough day, with my pain sentencing me to the couch. I told my dad I was feeling down, that I was sure my children would grow up resenting me because I couldn't play with blocks with them on the floor. I was just so tired—so tired that I hadn't had the energy to vacuum my house in nearly two weeks. My father consoled me the best he could and then hung up the phone.

About twenty minutes later there was a knock on our little apartment door. It was my dad, standing there smiling, holding his vacuum. With just a few words and a tender smile, he came in, sat me back down on the couch, and proceeded to vacuum my entire apartment.

A vacuum cleaner had never sounded sweeter.

I lay on the couch, watching my dad slowly and methodically push the vacuum up and back in perfect, loving straight lines. Each line was a symbol of my father's love for me. Each line was proof that my Father in Heaven had heard my prayers and had answered them through my father on earth.

When he was finished, my dad carefully coiled up the vacuum cord, gave me a hug, and went home.

He probably doesn't even remember that day, but I always will. It wasn't what he did, but why and how. A simple vacuuming, without fanfare or complaint, was his expression of love for me. My heart needed that love even more than my floors needed to be cleaned. I felt my father's love for me that day, and I felt my Father's love for me, too.

There is a sweet humility that brings us closer to God as we accept His help through the hands of others. It not only helps us but it also gives others the opportunity to grow closer to Him as they serve. He expects us to give them the chance to serve and to give Him the chance to show His love for us through them.

Paul wrote, "For we are labourers together with God" (1 Corinthians 3:9). I know that is what He wants: for us to labor and serve one another—and to be served—together.

Expectation 7: God expects you to seek knowledge.

This is one of my favorite topics. I believe that knowledge truly is power. The more you know, the clearer your vision, the greater your opportunities, the broader your horizons will be. God intends us to seek out knowledge (Proverbs 4:5, 7, 13), and He is willing to share with us His knowledge as soon as we are ready.

Hannah of the Old Testament was a faithful woman who loved the Lord. In a prayer of thanksgiving she said, "The Lord is a God of knowledge" (1 Samuel 2:3). She knew the Lord possesses all knowledge, and she turned to Him for guidance, help, and answers.

Her son, Samuel, did the same. One night, the Lord called to him. Samuel replied, "Speak; for thy servant heareth" (1 Samuel 3:10). The Lord tutored Samuel from the moment Samuel showed a willing heart—and a willing ear. "And Samuel grew, and the Lord was with him, and did let none of his words fall to the ground" (1 Samuel 3:19).

Prophets have interpreted the last phrase of that verse to mean that the Lord honored His prophet, Samuel, and fulfilled the prophecies he spoke (Old Testament student manual, 269). I like to imagine it from another point of view as well: that "his words" refers to the words the Lord gave to Samuel. Those words were so precious in Samuel's eyes that he clung to them tightly in his heart and, for Samuel, they did not fall to the ground unheeded.

What beautiful imagery that creates for me.

Think of the things that are precious to you that you would not allow to fall to the ground: your great-grandmother's china, your wedding ring, the last doughnut (those are precious). These are things you hold dear, things you would not want to lose. Such are the drops of knowledge that come from the Lord.

I am speaking of spiritual and wholesome secular knowledge. We need to become students of the scriptures, and we need to seek the best books on topics that are worthy of our time. We need to obtain a sound understanding of the world around us—science, math, economy, and politics (D&C 88:77–79, 118)—so that we may make good contributions to society.

Knowledge is important because, coupled with our faith, it gives direction to our desires.

There is a story of a loyal knight who was fiercely devoted to the good lord of the castle. One day the lord left on business. The knight, wanting to show his devotion, went to the west and destroyed the nearest village. When the lord returned, the knight said, "Lord, I have gone to the west and vanquished thine enemies in thine honor." He bowed and presented the lord with the spoils of his victory.

The lord kindly nodded to his knight and said, "Your devotion is noted, good knight. However, my enemies do not live to the west. They are to the east."

The point is that enthusiasm without direction can be dangerous.

Knowledge—righteous knowledge—gives us the proper direction for our enthusiasm and efforts. We know whose side we are on, and we know how we can best fight the good fight. As we gain more knowledge, we progress from being a pocketknife, so to speak, to being a multi-tool in the Lord's hands that can be used for a great many purposes.

In addition, we know that the knowledge we gain in this life will go with us to the next. Since our eternal progression extends beyond this life, it is reasonable that any knowledge we obtain here will give us a greater advantage there (D&C 130:18–19).

Heavenly Father gave us minds so that we may think for ourselves. We can decide what to believe, what to study, what to learn. I don't think He would give us a gift if He did not expect us to use it. He expects us to gain knowledge and to share the knowledge we gain with our families, friends, neighbors, coworkers, and others He might place in our paths. Like Ammon, we can be "wise, yet harmless" (Alma 18:22) as we use our knowledge for good.

Expectation 8: God expects you to have joy.

I'll be the first to admit that it's hard for me to be happy when someone takes the parking spot I've been waiting for or when one of my kids eats the last cookie and leaves the empty box in the pantry or when the dog runs through the house with muddy paws. I'm really not laughing then.

Seriously, though, life can be filled with difficult trials: illness, natural disasters, the loss of a job or a family member. Our Perspective can be tested and our patience tried. I have cried myself to sleep many times, wetting my pillow with tears of heartache and pain.

Nevertheless, I know that God intends for us to have joy in this life. Isaiah taught that "with joy shall ye draw water out of the wells of salvation" (Isaiah 12:3). James wrote, "Behold, we count them happy which endure" (James 5:11). In his final counsel, a dying Lehi reminded his family that "men are, that they might have joy" (2 Nephi 2:25). God wants to be happy and have joy.

What God means by "joy" is most likely different from the happiness we find in the world. Does He expect us to be giddy when the tough times come? Of course not. His joy is a small word with a grand meaning. In God's joy there is Perspective. In His joy there is confidence in the outcome, no matter what problems may arise. His joy magnifies the good and righteous things in life. We find deeper joy because we see deeper meaning in our lives and purpose in our trials.

I have a dear friend who has what I call a "perma-grin." He is always smiling and always joyful. I asked him how he does it, and he said, "What's not to be happy about?" I love that attitude! I have another friend, though, who is unhappy much of the time. She is always "waiting for the other shoe to fall," for the next bad thing to happen. She has a hard time finding joy, even in good times.

This makes me think of the first time I attempted to water-ski. It was in the days before I had children or stretch marks. Some friends invited my husband and me out on their boat for the day. They had all water-skied before and were eager to coach and encourage me.

I watched each of them start off in the water, hold on to the rope as the boat picked up speed, and get pulled up onto their skis. They swerved and sloshed, jumping and skimming smoothly behind the boat. Their seemingly effortless examples gave me the courage to try.

My heart was pumping hard as I bobbed in the water, skis strapped to my feet and the rope in my wet and shaking hands. I gave them the thumbs-up to indicate I was ready. "Three, two, one!" was the warning I heard before I began to be pulled, first slowly . . . then faster . . . and faster.

Water rushed up my nose while the skis, which had promised me so much fun, now took on their role as my enemy. My legs began to stretch apart under the force of the water, one to the east and the other to the west. My swimsuit began to ride up.

I let go of the rope.

It took a few minutes of treading water for me to catch my breath, but I was certain now: Water-skiing was of the devil.

My friends encouraged me to try again. Now, I believe in the "try and try again" mentality, but not when it comes to getting a nasal flush with salt water.

My options were severely limited, however, when I realized they were not going to allow me back in the boat until I "water-skied properly." So I did what any normal person would do—I yelled at them. Then, when I realized that resistance was futile, I grabbed the rope and gave them a very hesitant and slightly bitter thumbs-up.

Water came rushing into my nose again, my legs strained, and my swimsuit climbed. Each wave seemed to crash into me and push me down. I was tired, and I let go again. This same cycle went on for nearly an hour. I would try and fail and then try again—over and over.

Finally, the magic moment came. With just the right mixture of strength, skill, and luck, I pulled myself up out of the vicious water and onto my skis. Glory and triumph! I was water-skiing! I effortlessly zoomed across the top of the water. I hadn't realized how fast and smooth it could be, how free I could feel! What a difference from the struggle in the water!

It was wonderful. It was fast. It was smooth. I felt the wind rushing through my wet hair and the spray from the boat's wake on my body. Then suddenly I realized it was too fast and too smooth. At that speed, I could really hurt myself. I began to imagine the worst. I was going to crash and die at the first bump in the wake—I just knew it. No more than ten seconds after my triumphant emergence, I let go of the rope. I crashed into the water, hurting my body and my pride. I hadn't stayed up long enough to improve or even to enjoy myself. I was too focused on the bad things that might happen.

Life can be hard—really hard—at times. It may feel as though trials are tearing us apart and the pressure is just too great. It seems impossible to find any joy in the face of such strong opposition. We want to give up—we want to let go.

Other times, things can be going our way and we have the possibility of being truly happy—but we can't seem to enjoy it. We may sabotage these good times with guilt because others are struggling and we are not or with fear that something bad will inevitably happen. We succumb to feelings of unworthiness and doubt. Eventually we let go of the joy and allow ourselves to return to a state of struggle because it is what is familiar and, in a strange way, comfortable to us.

My adventure in water-skiing wasn't a life-changing event, but the lessons I learned from it were. When life is tough and you are fighting just to stay above water—keep fighting. When you finally make it to the top, enjoy it, embrace it, and remember it. There will be an end to the smooth and fantastic ride, but that's life. Don't let the ride end because you let go. Most important, when you find yourself back down in the water, take a deep breath and find the strength do it all over again. Find joy in knowing that you can.

When our Perspective is good, our life seems better, and our joy can be real.

Expectation 9: God expects you to overcome and triumph.

I love this one because I know that God has faith in me—I have faith in *Him*, but I also know that *He* has faith in *me*. He knows I can overcome. He expects nothing less, because He knows I can do it. The Lord said to Nephi, "Follow me, and do the things which ye have seen me do" (2 Nephi 31:12). There wasn't an "even though I don't think you can do it" at the end of the verse. That call is to all of us because He knows we can do it.

I cannot tell you how strong and powerful that makes me feel.

If God tells me I can do it, then I must accept that. God is perfect—He cannot lie. Therefore, I *must* be able to do anything He asks me to do.

I often think of Mary, the mother of Jesus, as she received the angelic news of her sacred calling. She did not express doubt that she could do it; she only wondered how it was going to happen.

In response to her wonderment, the angelic messenger said, "For with God nothing shall be impossible." That was good enough for her. She responded, "Behold the handmaid of the Lord; be it unto me according to thy word" (Luke 1:37–38).

Mary had complete faith in God—and in His faith in her. Keep in mind that Mary and her people knew of the coming of the Savior—it had been prophesied for hundreds of years. This was no small thing God was asking of her. This would be the most significant event ever to happen—until the Atonement that would be performed by her son and Savior—and yet she knew that if God asked her to do it, she could.

Mary knew that through God all things truly are possible. She humbly said, "My soul doth magnify the Lord" (Luke 1:46).

Paul understood this principle, as well. In a letter to the Romans he said, "We are more than conquerors through him that loved us" (Romans 8:37). And in a letter to the Philippians he said, "I can do all things through Christ which strengtheneth me" (Philippians 4:13).

Believe that God will not give you a trial you cannot overcome. I know that He did not set you up to fail. His entire work is to bring about your success. The emotional mountains that may seem insurmountable to us may be summited with the right help and the right equipment. He has given us what we need to be triumphant: agency, the light of Christ, inspiration from the Holy Ghost, commandments, scriptures, prophets, ordinances such as baptism, people He places in our lives, and so much more.

He has the power to help us succeed. His Son has the power to save. Together we have the power to overcome.

Armed with a deeper understanding of your relationship with your Heavenly Father and what He wants for you, coupled with your newfound Perspective, you have the ability to see yourself as you really are. You can feel secure and confident in yourself and in your purpose. It doesn't matter how the world defines you, what your neighbors think of you, or how anyone else views you, for that matter. You know that God is your Father in Heaven. You know that He loves you. You know Jesus Christ is your Savior and that He died for you. You know that God has already made plans for you to succeed and that He expects you to triumph. You can stand in quiet confidence and love for yourself because you can see yourself as He does.

This confidence then places you in more situations where God can use you for His purposes. You have graduated to becoming a bona fide multi-tool in His hands. When He looks upon His children and sees a task that needs to be accomplished, you can answer with confidence: "Here am I, send me" (Isaiah 6:8; Abraham 3:27). You will have no fear and no doubt because you know God, you love Him, and you have faith in Him. You know that He knows you, loves you, and has faith in you, too.

That's the power of Perspective.

Chapter Four

heavenly bifocals

Seeing the Deeper Purpose in Our Trials

All these things shall give thee experience,
and shall be for thy good.
Doctrine and Covenants 122:7

Perspective allows us not only to see ourselves in a clearer, more pure light but also to more clearly see the world around us—and that can be a very valuable thing. As we have mentioned, life can be really hard. Sometimes we are required to go through things that nearly break us, things that may cause us to question whether God even knows we're alive. I assure you once again that He does know you're alive, and He very much cares about what happens to you.

Many times we bring pain upon ourselves through our poor choices. Some of that pain can be assuaged by making better decisions. Other times we might suffer because of the choices of others. And there are yet other times when we struggle because God allows us to experience things such as natural disasters, illness, and loss. Much of this kind of pain can't be avoided—it's just a part of life.

Some may question why we have to experience certain trials or why God allows us to hurt. In the book of James we find this counsel: "Count it all joy when ye fall into many afflictions; knowing this, that the trying of your faith worketh patience. But let patience have her perfect work, that ye may be perfect and entire, wanting [or lacking] nothing" (JST James 1:2–4). "Perfect" means "complete, finished, fully developed" (Matthew 5:48*b*). As we work through our afflictions in patience and faith, we draw near to God and become more complete, finished, and fully developed—eventually becoming like Him.

My oldest daughter works on a farm in exchange for leasing a horse. One day she and I were grooming her horse together. She was quietly brushing one side of the horse, and I was brushing the other. We were listening to the music on the radio when suddenly she popped her head above the horse's haunches and said, "You know, Mom, bonding with a horse isn't in the victory—it's in the grooming."

Intrigued by her burst of inspiration, I asked to her explain.

"Well," she said, brushing a horse hair off her cheek, "some people think that you bond with a horse after you cross the finish line, when everyone is yelling and patting her on the back and telling her she did a good job. That's nice and all, but the real bonding is what happens here, in the barn. It's the small things—the brushing, picking the hooves, the touching, and the talking. That's when you bond with the horse—when you're taking care of it."

Although she didn't realize it at the time, my daughter had shared a profound insight about life. Many people look forward to the end, when the race of life is finished and they can be with God again, as if that's when they will bond with Him. But I don't think that is the case.

Our trials are opportunities not only to prove ourselves but also to bond with our Father as He cares for us. The bonding comes as He grooms, or prepares and refines, us. Some of that grooming takes place when life seems to be running smoothly, but much of it happens smack-dab in the middle of our trials. It happens as the brush in our Master's hand smooths out the tangles in our lives or in the way He picks out our weaknesses and makes them strengths. It happens in the small moments when He touches our hearts or when we can hear Him speak to us.

Perspective allows us to see His hand in our life, grooming us, loving us, caring for us. Perspective permits us to trust that God will not give us more than we can handle. Perspective helps us to understand that even though we can see only a piece of the big picture right now, we can have faith in the One who created it. Perspective assures us that we are not alone in our trials. Perspective enables us to see the purpose in pain—even when it is a difficult thing for us, and for God, to experience.

With Perspective we can be confident in ourselves through our trials, even when we are stuck in an elevator.

The Elevator Called Me Fat: No More Than We Can Handle

On the surface, elevators don't bother me, but underneath—yes, I do have issues with them. Maybe as a child I was frightened by Willy Wonka's glass elevator. Or perhaps I was influenced by every action movie in the '80s where people were stuck in elevators or crawling on top of elevators or the elevator's cables were breaking and threatening to dash everyone inside to pieces.

One day I was waiting with a group of people to get on an elevator. As the doors opened, our group began to file inside. I was one of the last ones waiting to get on, and I could see it was pretty full. I stood back with one other woman and motioned for the group to go on without us, telling them we would catch the next elevator. After a little maneuvering and cajoling, the group convinced us there was enough room for us.

The other woman went on first, and then I followed, squeezing into a small opening between two very large men. Then the doors closed—but the elevator didn't move.

We stared at each other while someone pressed the button again. Nothing.

Suddenly the doors opened up again. A feminine voice blasted through the overhead speakers straight into my heart: *"Weight overload. There is too much weight on this elevator. Weight overload."*

I could not believe it. My cheeks flushed, and I thought, "The elevator just called me fat."

Red-faced, I made a lame joke about eating brownies for breakfast and sheepishly walked off the elevator and back into the lobby. I caught the next elevator and was greeted by the rest of the group when I reached the fifth floor. They were laughing. I wasn't.

I share this harrowing experience with you to shed light on a truth that is vital to our Perspective: *God will not give us trials that are too heavy for us to bear.*

The elevator has a built-in system that does not allow the load to exceed a certain weight. This prevents wear and tear and damage to the elevator mechanism. It assures that the elevator functions properly and passengers are kept safe.

We, like elevators, carry loads every day. Sometimes the load is light, and other times the load is heavy. Sometimes the load seems too great for us to bear. Heavenly Father has a system that does not allow us to carry a load that is too heavy or to be tried beyond what we can handle. "God is faithful," Paul said, "who will not suffer you to be tempted [or tried] above that ye are able" (1 Corinthians 10:13).

God has promised that He will not allow us to become overburdened to the point of immobility and failure. He is "mindful of every people . . . and his bowels of mercy are over all the earth" (Alma 26:37). He is keenly aware of us, and He will not give us more than we have strength to carry. No matter what burdens we bear today, right now, He knows we can handle it—because He will help us.

The key is that we must rely on our Heavenly Father and our Savior to help with the load—not only the heavy ones but also the lighter ones. Jesus said, "Come unto me, all ye that labour and are heavy laden, and I will give you rest. . . . For my yoke is easy and my burden is light" (Matthew 11:28–30). When we feel heavy laden, we can know that with His help we can handle our burdens, and our ability and capacity to bear them will be greater.

I still have issues with elevators—especially if they try to call me fat—but I do find comfort in the knowledge that whatever load I am asked to carry, God will give me the strength to do it. That knowledge also gives me confidence, and confidence boosts my strength even more.

A Small Part: See the Big Picture

Even though we understand that we will not be given more than we can handle, it is still a natural longing to understand *why* a certain trial is taking place. Why am I asked to carry this load or bear this burden? Why me? Why now? We may ask these questions, especially when a tragedy occurs that simply does not make sense to us.

I was talking to a woman who was preparing a birthday party for her little girl. She had a myriad of activities for the guests to do during the four-hour bash. During one of the activities she would present pictures of things around the house—light fixtures, a couch, books, and so forth—and the girls would run around trying to identify the items.

That doesn't sound too difficult—until you hear that the pictures she gave them were close-ups, revealing only a small part of each of the items. She commented that things look completely different when you see only a piece of them and that it would be a challenge for the girls to find the correct items from only partial pictures.

The same thing is true about our lives. It is sometimes difficult to recognize the purpose of life, especially its challenges, when we see only a piece of it—no matter how clearly we see that single piece. If we focus on the small pieces that are filled with sorrow, grief, loneliness, or pain, we lose the perspective of the whole purpose of life.

But when we take a step back and look at the big picture, we find meaning in our sorrows, our joys are magnified, and each day takes on a different light.

When we look at life with Perspective, we can also see that each of us plays a part in the big picture of God's plan for His children. We see how each person's life has purpose, how we are eternally symbiotic, how we are all here for the same purpose, regardless of color, station, or gender. We are all here to have a human experience.

Each piece of our lives gives us an opportunity to be tested and to prove ourselves; each moment gives us a chance to become a better person—to be more honest or courageous, to have more integrity, to be more patient or more humble, to love more.

When a piece of your life seems overwhelming and feels as if it is taking all of your focus, try to take a step back and consider that piece as part of your whole life experience. Take your trial, your job, your relationship, or whatever the piece may be, and try to understand that it is a part of something bigger. There is more to the picture than just the piece you see. There is more to the family you have. There is more to the trial you are going through. There is more to you.

Heavenly Father is near. You can ask Him to help you see the big picture, to help you find where your piece belongs, how it fits, what purposes it plays in the whole. As you work with your Father in Heaven and look at your life with Perspective, you can find peace and strength in each of your pieces, even the most trying ones.

He is Here:
Our Father and Our Savior Are Always Near

While we were visiting extended family in California, my sister-in-law became very ill. Her husband, my brother, was out of town, so she asked me to accompany her to the emergency room.

We arrived at the hospital around 8:00 p.m. The next two hours were filled with registration and testing—a merely tedious process for one who is pain-free, but it was excruciating for my sister-in-law, who was already in a lot of pain. During this time, we were relegated to a small bench in the packed, noisy waiting room.

We tried to reach my brother, who was a two-hour drive away at girls' camp. Because of poor reception on his end, we were unsuccessful in reaching him.

I tried to keep my sister-in-law's spirits up as we waited. I made faces and cracked jokes as we talked about life in general. After a couple of hours, though, her pain had worsened, and she became quiet and withdrawn.

Finally, I was able to reach my brother. I explained the situation—that his wife wasn't well, but she was doing all right. Although she hadn't been seen by a doctor yet, we were sure the situation wasn't life-threatening. I told him it wasn't necessary for him to come; his wife just wanted him to know what was going on. As (bad) luck would have it, when I reached him she was in a back room having her blood drawn and wasn't able to speak to him herself.

After a long while she returned to the waiting room. It had been nearly three hours since we had arrived at the hospital. She was relieved to learn that I had finally reached her husband. Just knowing that he was aware of her and that he cared lifted her spirits.

I continued my attempts to lift her spirits, but as the evening turned into night I could tell that worry and fatigue were setting in.

Her condition was getting worse. Just then, her phone rang. It was her husband. They spoke only briefly, and then she turned to me with wide eyes and said, "He left camp as soon as he got off the phone with you—he's almost here."

We weren't expecting him to come, but the thought of his impending arrival gave her a second wind—even if all she could muster was a small smile between winces.

The next forty minutes were filled with light conversation as we took turns watching the hospital doors open and shut. Each time, her eyes lit up at the possibility of seeing her husband walk through the doors. But each time, it was instead some other unfortunate creature who needed to be taken care of.

She began to feel discouraged. I could see that she was losing strength and hope. She was tired, and she admitted she was frightened.

It was at that moment, nearly four hours after we arrived at the emergency room, that the door opened once more. I looked up and saw my brother walk into the waiting room.

"He is here," I said.

She stood as quickly as she could, and their eyes met. The expression on each of their faces was tender and raw. Her eyes watered, and she smiled the kind of smile that encompassed love, joy, fear and relief. *He is here.*

He smiled as well, but his smile was different from hers. It was filled with love, but it also held reassurance and caring. Even though he had not been with her during those previous hours, his expression was somehow knowing—as though by simply looking at her he understood what she had been through.

It was a sweet reunion.

After they embraced, my brother sat down beside us. We talked for a while until I felt completely out of place. All they wanted and needed was each other. I knew it was time for me to go, and I left, knowing that no matter what happened that night, she would be all right—because he was there.

I have often thought of that night, and I cannot help but see in it a sweet illustration of our relationship with our Heavenly Father.

There are times in our lives when we aren't doing well, when we are hurting. We try to put on a brave face. We try to make the right choices, be in the right places, say the right things. We get help from our family and friends. Sometimes, even when we are surrounded by loved ones, even when we are doing all that we should be doing, we still feel pain. We feel tired, we feel scared, and we feel alone.

So we pray and we plead. Sometimes it feels as though relief will never come.

But He is here. He is full of love, hope, and peace. He does know what we have been through.

The zenith event of the Book of Mormon is the Savior's appearance after His resurrection to the people who lived on the American continent. The people were gathered at the temple in Bountiful and were conversing about the signs they had witnessed concerning Jesus' death. They had experienced turmoil, sorrow, and heavy hearts. And then He came. His descent from above was preceded by a heavenly introduction that penetrated their very hearts. They still did not fully comprehend who and what they were seeing, and as the Savior stood before them, they "durst not open their mouths, even one to another" (3 Nephi 11:8).

Then He stretched out his hand and spoke: "Behold, I am Jesus Christ, whom the prophets have testified shall come into the world" (3 Nephi 11:9–10). When they realized the prophecy was coming to pass—that Jesus Christ had come to show Himself to them—the multitude fell to their knees. *He is here.*

The Savior then allowed the people—2,500 of them (3 Nephi 17:25)—to come to Him one by one and feel with their own hands the prints of the nails in His hands and His feet and gaze upon Him with their own eyes. They rejoiced in unison, and, overcome with emotion, they fell at His feet and worshipped Him (3 Nephi 11:9–17). *He is here.* The resurrected Lord stayed among the people, teaching them, blessing them, praying for them, weeping for them, and loving them. The memory of that sacred and momentous appearance kept peace and hope alive among the people of the Book of Mormon for two hundred years.

My sister-in-law didn't see her husband come into the waiting room that night because her head hung down with fatigue. It was when she looked up and saw him that everything changed.

He is here. Although the Lord might not be physically present in our rooms, in our homes, at work, or standing next to us, He is here in spirit, in purpose, in reality. We simply need to look up to see Him. He knows what we are feeling. He knows our intentions. He knows our joys. He knows our talents. He knows our pains. He knows us and loves us. It is up to us to look up and really see Him. And when we do, everything will change.

He brings hope, peace, love, joy, strength, and empathy. When we don't think we can go on—and even when we think we can and we don't need Him—He is here, and we are not alone.

Lucy's Hands: Purpose to Our Pain

It helps to know we won't be given more than we can handle, that our vision allows us to see only a small part of God's big picture, and that we are not alone. But even so, we might still want to know *why* we must endure some of the burdens we are asked to bear.

I used to ask, "Why?" until a young mother's example answered the question for me.

One Sunday, I was walking down the hallway to teach my class of five-year-olds when a sister stopped me. She told me that Lucy, the sweet, almost-one-year-old daughter of a friend of mine, had been taken to the hospital. No one knew exactly what had happened, only that Lucy had been hurt.

By the end of our Sunday meetings, most of the congregation had been made aware of the situation. Meals were scheduled to be taken to the home. Care for Lucy's older brother had been arranged. Prayers had already been whispered. Some tears had already been shed.

Through phone calls and visits, we learned what had happened. Lucy had been playing on the floor as her family was getting ready for church. They had just moved into a new home, and Lucy was exploring the new family room. She was just beginning to walk and would often hold on to furniture and other things to help herself stand. This particular morning, Lucy crawled over to the gas fireplace and pulled herself to a standing position, leaning her full weight on her small hands as they pressed into the pane of hot glass. The heat was intense, but Lucy was too young to realize that the palms of her hands were burning. She simply stood there, leaning against the hot glass for several seconds before her mother saw her and ran across the room.

Lucy's quick-thinking parents immediately sought medical care. It was a long day of tears, doctors, praying, and waiting.

After a few days in the hospital, Lucy was able to come home. My husband and I paid the family a visit. Lucy was already in bed, and we sat with her parents, Matt and Stephanie, who were understandably exhausted. As we listened to them retell their experience, I was moved by their faith in the face of this adversity. My heart ached when they told me of the pain and suffering Lucy had experienced. I thought to myself how grateful I was that the ordeal was over—Lucy was home now, safe and warm in bed.

Then her mother told me about Lucy's recovery process.

The doctors had performed skin grafts to save her hands. Then,

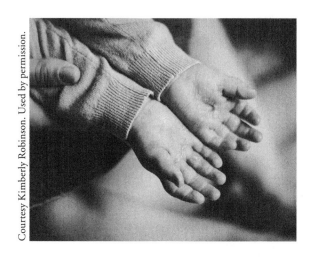

Courtesy Kimberly Robinson. Used by permission.

to protect them as they healed, her hands and arms were wrapped up to the elbows. During the healing process, the palms of Lucy's hands would need to be stretched to prevent the skin from healing too tightly. Stephanie smiled through tired, moist eyes as she explained to my husband and me that this stretching had to be done not once or twice a day but every hour.

"Does it hurt?" I asked.

The answer was a tearful "Yes, but it's the only way for her hands to heal correctly." If the palms weren't stretched, the skin would not heal with enough flexibility, and Lucy would not be able to open her hands fully as she grew older. *We have to be stretched to grow.*

Oh, this poor little girl! was my first thought. To endure not only such initial pain and trauma but to have to experience pain over and over again—how heartbreaking!

The following Sunday, I saw Stephanie and Lucy in the restroom at church. It was time for the hourly stretching of Lucy's hands. I watched as Stephanie set her smiling little girl on the counter and talked softly to her. Then she gently took Lucy's hand. Lucy recoiled and began to whimper, knowing what was about to happen. Calmly and gently, Stephanie bent Lucy's fingers back to stretch the healing skin. Lucy cried.

Stephanie spoke the tender words of a loving parent: "I know it hurts. I'm sorry. We are almost finished. You are doing so well. Mommy's right here. I love you." I turned my head and looked at the floor, feeling that I was invading a private moment between mother and daughter. I was also trying to hide my tears. I was watching a painful yet tender exchange between child and parent. But it struck me that I was also witnessing a profound representation of the relationship between me and my heavenly Parent.

There have been many times in my life when I have struggled or when I have felt tired and stretched. In my younger days, my prayers often included this plea: "Heavenly Father, how can you let this happen to me?" It was difficult for me to understand how so much pain could be for my benefit. I thought that if God loved me, He would save me from it. But most of the time that did not happen.

Little Lucy hurt herself—even though she was not fully aware of what she was doing—and she had loving parents who helped her heal. Even though it hurt, they knew that stretching her hands would lead to full use of them in the future. *Temporary pain now would lead to full recovery later.* Her parents knew this, so they stretched her hands for her benefit, even though it broke their hearts to do it. Out of their deep love for their daughter and their understanding of how necessary the stretching was, they not only allowed Lucy to hurt but they willingly and lovingly acted as the instigators of the pain. It took great courage and emotional strength on their part to administer this therapy, but they did what was hard *now* in order to help Lucy in the long run.

It might have been easier for them to say, "No, we don't want Lucy to hurt anymore. She's been through enough. We want to protect her. We will not stretch her hands." But they were looking at the situation through the eyes of loving parents. They were looking at and loving not just the little Lucy but also the Lucy of the future: Lucy the future piano player, Lucy the future mother, Lucy the future artist, Lucy with full use of her hands. They understood the difficult truth that Lucy would have to endure pain now to reach a greater potential later.

We are told that the purpose of our mortal existence is that we might have joy (2 Nephi 2:25), but our lives in mortality are also punctuated with all manner of trials and tribulations. During these difficult times, we might feel stretched; we might feel pain and even suffering. We might cry as Alma did, when he was bound, imprisoned, and beaten, "How long shall we suffer these great afflictions, O Lord?" (Alma 14:26).

When we feel stretched and are suffering, we might find ourselves wishing that our Heavenly Father would say, "No, I don't want you to hurt anymore. You've been through enough. I want to protect you. I will not stretch you anymore." If that wish were granted, we would momentarily be free from pain or discomfort. We might feel relief and happiness. It might seem to be an easier way to end the trial—but we would not grow.

Alma had faith, even in the midst of his afflictions. His plea to know how long the suffering would last was immediately followed by, "O Lord, give us strength according to our faith which is in Christ unto deliverance" (Alma 14:26). Alma understood that faith was imperative in the face of adversity. He knew that the Lord had a purpose and a plan for him, and he looked to God for guidance and help.

Our Father in Heaven loves us dearly and perfectly. He does not find any joy in our suffering. But He is not looking at and loving us just for the present. He is also looking at and loving our future selves. He knows that sometimes healing hurts. He knows that for us to grow, we need to be stretched. He knows that for us to become like Jesus Christ, we need to change, and sometimes change comes only through adversity.

As a loving parent himself, Alma later testified of this principle to his son. He said, "I have been supported under trials and troubles of every kind, yea, and all manner of afflictions; . . . and I do put my trust in him, and he will still deliver me" (Alma 36:27).

What a powerful example Lucy's family was, to me and to the entire congregation, of the influence of the love of good parents—and our Heavenly Parent. It reminds me there is purpose to my suffering. It also helps me to understand that my Father in Heaven allows me to suffer because He loves me—and that it is not an easy thing for Him to allow. It gives me hope that I can be healed, that pain is only temporary. And it helps me know that my loving Heavenly Father is there for me throughout the trial *and* the healing.

I am reminded of the gentle words that Lucy heard from her loving mother during the painful stretching: "I know it hurts. I'm sorry. We are almost finished. You are doing so well. Mommy's right here. I love you. You will be okay."

Now, when I am hurting, feeling stretched, and growing, I imagine those words as an earthly echo of my Heavenly Father's loving message to me: "I know it hurts. I'm sorry. We are almost finished. You are doing so well. I am right here, and I love you. You will be okay." We know we are loved not because our life is easy but because He is there to help us when it is hard.

That's the power of Perspective.

Perspective helps us find solace in the truth that God will not give us more than we can handle. Perspective helps us understand that even though we see only a piece of the big picture we can still have faith in the One who created it. Perspective assures us that we are not alone in our trials and enables us to find the purpose in our lives and in our pain.

With Perspective, we can be confident—even if an elevator calls us fat.

Now that we are armed with an eternal Perspective, and now that we have learned to see ourselves and our lives more clearly, we can move on to the next exciting part: choosing to be.

PART TWO

choose to be

ice cream and choices

Discover, Decide, and Become Who You Can Be

*May you realize that in you is the control of your life and
what you are going to be, what you are going to do.*
Spencer W. Kimball

Children are often asked, "What do you want to be when you grow up?" The answer may be that he or she wants to be a fireman, a policeman, a teacher, an animal doctor, or even the president. Whatever they answer, we smile back and tell them, "That's great!" We assure them that if they really try, they can be whatever they want to be. Perhaps we don't believe it entirely, but we say it because we want *them* to believe it.

Time, choices, and circumstances may have dimmed our own hope and confidence that we can be whatever we want to be, but we still want our children to believe in that dream. We want them to have the joy that comes from hope and the opportunities that come from confidence. So we smile, encourage, lead, and teach—and hope they can be whoever they really want to be.

In Part One of this book, we discussed learning how to see: how to see yourself, God, and life through His eyes. I hope this Perspective has given you the hope and confidence that I believe God wants you to have. He knows who you can be and what you can accomplish when you see things as He sees them.

Now, in Part Two, we will discuss choosing to be who you want to be—more precisely, who God knows and wants you to be. By now you've seen that Perspective is one of my favorite words. In this chapter we'll encounter another of my favorite words—*choice*—and the life-changing power it brings. We'll explore the value of choice, how we make our choices, choosing who we want to be and what we believe, and, finally, acting on our choices to magnify ourselves through God's guidance.

Play-Doh: Choices Mold Our Lives

I love Play-Doh. I love the smell, the feel, and, yes, even the taste (its salty, grainy texture was a culinary favorite of mine when I was five).

Play-Doh elicits creativity, from the rolling of an uneven worm to the creation of a masterpiece. I particularly love brand-new Play-Doh fresh out of the can. It's perfect and untouched. The color is pure, and the texture is soft and pliable. It begs to be used, and I can make anything I want.

I don't love old Play-Doh, though. The once-vibrant colors become a faded purplish-gray mass with remnants of yellow, blue, green, red, and white. If I leave it out of the can, it becomes crusty and not pliable. It is hard to work with—monochromatic and stiff. I have made it impossible to create what I want.

You've heard the saying, "Like putty in my hands." When we hold brand-new Play-Doh in our hands, we see it through childlike eyes; we see it not for what it is, but for what its possibilities are. Have you ever seen a child open a new can of Play-Doh and exclaim, "Wow! I'm gonna put this away and never touch it"? No, they invariably pull out the tube of clay and mash it into a ball or a pancake. The more ardent Play-Doh artists might create a piggy, a pretzel, or a doughnut (which they might actually try to eat). But no matter what the creation, or how old or skilled the craftsman is, the same desire is there: to turn the cylindrical lump into something more.

In matters of self, we share that same innate drive to create something more, to be something more. We came here as brand-new little human beings, and during our lives we are molded into the people we are today. Some of us like who we are and some of us don't. Some of us have lost the vision of who we wanted to be. Some of us—dare I say, a great majority of us—either have lost or never had the vision of who our Heavenly Father knew we could be.

The beauty of having an eternal Perspective is that it helps you know that the molding process is never finished. With Perspective, you can see your worth and potential. You know that you are a daughter of the God that created the universe, and you have His divine DNA. He has a purpose and a plan for you, and He knows who you can be and what you can accomplish. With Perspective, you know He adores you, has faith in you, trusts you, and has complete confidence in you. You understand that at this very moment He is working on your behalf, overseeing people and situations and opportunities and circumstances that can help you learn, grow, and succeed. You know what makes you special and where your worth comes from. You know you have a lot to give—not only of yourself, but of God's goodness through you.

When we have Perspective, we know we can decide who and what we want to be and that through our choices we can make it happen. Through every righteous decision we make and through every righteous action that stems from those decisions, we can mold ourselves into the person our Father knows we can be.

Conversely, through our unrighteous choices we can mold ourselves into more selfish, angry, or resentful people. We can either keep ourselves fresh and pliable like new Play-Doh, or we can become discolored and crusty like old Play-Doh.

We are not the same person from day to day. The choices we made yesterday mold us into who we are today, and our choices today will mold the person we will be tomorrow. For some, the change is almost imperceptible; for others, it is the difference between night and day. We are who we are because of our choices. *We are the sum of our choices and what we allow ourselves to become.*

The good news is that if we don't like the person we have allowed ourselves to become, either through unrighteous choices or through surrendering to the Enemies of Perspective, we are only one choice away from starting anew. With Perspective and the Savior's Atonement, we have the blessed opportunity to "reshape" our lives as we would new Play-Doh. And if we do like who we are, we can always be greater—and there is power and beauty in knowing that our choices can help us retain our goodness as we progress toward perfection.

Ask yourself these questions: "Who do I want to be?" "How close am I right now to being that person?" and finally, "What choice can I make right now to get me closer to being the person I want to be?"

After you have pondered these questions, you have one simple thing to do: *make a choice.* It doesn't have to be a big one. A small one will do. Just make one. Begin to mold yourself into someone spectacular. With the help of Heavenly Father and through the power of Perspective, you can be the person that your Father and your Savior intend you to be.

We have the power to mold ourselves into worms or masterpieces. We have the right to be confident, to be bold, to be happy, and to be tools in His hands—but *we must choose* to be those things. Just because we have the right doesn't mean we automatically reap the rewards. When we understand who we really are and how He really sees us, the doors of opportunity, growth, and peace are open to us, but we have to decide to act. We can be molded only if we allow Him to do the molding.

Realizing our potential is not enough. We must choose to become.

If: The Power of Agency

If—along with Perspective and Choice—has become one of my favorite words. It is the small hinge on the giant door of our lives. Within its two little letters, important principles such as accountability, responsibility, possibility, and the power to choose can be found. In that short word lie the power of opportunity and potential reward.

In the New Testament we read of a woman who had "an issue of blood." As Jesus passed through the streets of the city, this woman saw Him and knew that He had the power to heal her. She had Perspective, but that wasn't enough for her. Her Perspective compelled her to act.

She thought, "*If* I may touch but his clothes, I shall be whole" (Mark 5:28; emphasis added). Notice that power word: *if*. She had faith in Christ, but she understood that she must act on her faith in order to reach her desired outcome—to be made whole. It was up to her.

What amazing faith she had! She chose to put her faith and trust in Jesus into action. She reached out from behind Him and touched the hem of His robe—and she was healed.

In speaking of faith, Jesus taught that "*if* ye have faith as a grain of mustard seed, . . . nothing shall be impossible to you" (Matthew 17:20; emphasis added). Faith is a spiritual gift—a gift from God—but neither Heavenly Father nor Jesus will force us to act on our faith. It is truly up to us. The power to access faith, the blessings of the Atonement, and our potential is in our hands if we choose to act.

The Savior often used the word *If* in His teachings:

"If any man will come after me, let him deny himself and take up his cross daily and follow me" (Luke 9:32; emphasis added).

"If any man will do his will, he shall know of the doctrine, whether it be of God, or whether I speak of myself" (John 7:17; emphasis added).

"If ye know these things, happy are ye *if* ye do them" (John 13:17; emphasis added).

"If ye love me, keep my commandments" (John 14:15; emphasis added).

"Ye are my friends, *if* ye do whatsoever I command you" (John 15:13; emphasis added).

"Blessed are ye *if* ye shall keep the commandments" (3 Nephi 18:14; emphasis added).

If.

So many wonderful things may be ours—*if* we choose them.

If encapsulates the greatest gift that God has given us: our agency. From the time our first parents entered the Garden of Eden to our modern day, God has shown us the way and allowed us to choose for ourselves, to act and not be acted upon (2 Nephi 2:13).

Motivational author Stephen Covey taught that "between stimulus and response is our greatest power—the freedom to choose." Covey also outlined a few key principles we need to understand about our ability to choose. He taught that "our behavior is a function of our decisions, not our conditions" and that "it's not what happens to us, but our response to what happens to us that hurts us" (*7 Habits,* 70, 71, 73).

Understanding the *If* in our lives means that we accept the responsibility of it as well. We understand that we cannot place the blame for our condition or our happiness or unhappiness on society, our spouses, our circumstances, our genes, our environment, or anything else. We realize that when we do that, we are, in essence, saying that we have no control over what we say or what we do and that our choices and actions are caused by something or someone else. When we place blame on others, we shift to them the responsibility for our happiness. We trade our responsibility to pilot our own plane for the luxury of blaming someone else if it crashes.

But with Perspective, we know better. We know that we have a God-given right and responsibility to own every action and reaction we may have, every decision we make, every thought we have, and everything we say, because we own our own lives.

When you own your choices, you are no longer a victim of your circumstances but a navigator with purpose. You no longer let life happen to you—you make it happen. You no longer allow others to control you—you claim dominion over yourself. You take responsibility for who and where you are and what you do.

It sounds easier than it is, of course. Breaking free from the blame game can be difficult and actually quite scary. But it is important to understand that when you stand before the Lord to be judged, it will be just you and He. When He looks at the black spot of resentment on your heart, you cannot point to your husband and say, "Oh, that. Well, that's not my fault. You see, one day I told my husband that I wasn't going to diet anymore, that I was just going to try to eat healthy foods and exercise more and see where my body lands. Then he looked at me and said, 'I think your body already has landed.' Can you believe that? So, you see, that spot isn't my fault. It's obviously his."

That won't work.

We are responsible for who we are and who we will become. It might be a scary notion, but it's also an exciting one. *We can—and should—decide who and what we are and will be and how happy we will be.* C. Terry Warner, professor of philosophy at Brigham Young University, said, "The quality of life depends upon the choices we make, moment by moment, to do exactly what we sense is right toward all living things, including God" (*Bonds*, 319).

Knowing we have responsibility for ourselves may not be as scary when we realize that we are already pretty spectacular to begin with. Wanting to be "better" does not mean we are not "good enough" now. We are pretty amazing right now—but we can be more. Armed with His Perspective to see that, what remains is for us to choose from all the wonderful choices we have.

Ice Cream and Choices: Growth from Making Choices

When I was seventeen, I found my first job at an ice cream parlor, and I loved it. The employees got to eat as much free ice cream as they wanted—at least, that's what my nineteen-year-old supervisor told me. So, of course, I ate it. A lot of it. I loved ice cream, and I still do. But there were some things about the job I didn't love. Having to be there at a certain time and stay for the whole shift seemed suffocating to a free-spirited (and, arguably, lazy) teenager. I also didn't love smelling like a sack of sour milk at the end of each workday. How something so right could smell so wrong was a complete mystery to me.

The shop I worked for was known for its thirty-one flavors of ice cream. Each customer handled differently the decision of which flavor to choose. Sometimes people came into the store and knew just what they wanted. Others walked slowly back and forth, staring at each flavor, tasting each in their minds before they made a choice. Some would ask for recommendations, while others hemmed and hawed until everyone else had ordered, never able to make up their minds.

There was a little-known option that our store offered (I heard about this option from my nineteen-year-old supervisor, too): For the price of a single scoop of ice cream, you could have a taste of all thirty-one flavors. I'd seen only one person exercise this option, and it was quite a sight. The woman had a flavor in mind, but she couldn't make a decision, so, to help narrow down the choices, she opted to try all of them. She experienced a rainbow of taste, loving the chocolate and hating the sherbet. By the end of the thirty-one-flavor parade, it was time for her to decide. The poor woman was so full from all the samples that she left without ordering a full scoop of the flavor she had initially thought she wanted. She left feeling full but not satisfied.

I thought of this experience when I had a big decision to make. I had many options before me, but in the end I needed to choose one. How could I choose? Which would it be?

I tried the method of mentally walking down each path, imagining the different outcomes in my mind. None of them seemed undesirable—in fact, each of them had its advantages. That made it more difficult. Making a decision can be so much easier when one result is obviously bad and the other positively good—but this choice wasn't like that. It was a choice between good or good or good or good. I'll admit, it was tempting to skip the decision-making process altogether, but I knew that then I wouldn't be able to enjoy any of the possible outcomes.

I knew I had to pick something—I had to choose a path. But I was overwhelmed by the choices. I thought back to my ice cream parlor job once again. Sometimes when the customers couldn't decide, I would talk with them about the kinds of things they liked and didn't like and make a recommendation based on their preferences. I was confident in my ability to guide them because I, of course, had tasted every flavor in the store—most of them more than once. Most of the time, the customers loved my recommendations and were grateful for the outside help.

As I made my decision, I knew that I, too, had an outside source who could educate me about my choices—Heavenly Father.

Our Father in Heaven is the ultimate guide; He is the definitive resource to help us define our wants and our needs. He already knows all the choices before us—He may have placed them there. He expects us to do our part to make the most responsible, reasonable, and righteous decision. And He will help us do that. When we are torn between two choices or when we struggle to make the right one, He is the source to whom we should turn for direction.

I knew I would never experience the fullness of anything if I didn't choose a path, and, because I was not sure of myself, I asked for a recommendation. I turned to God and asked Him what He thought I should do. I had faith that He wanted me to be happy. I had the knowledge that He loved me. I had the hope that He would answer me. I had the peace of knowing I could ask Him. I had the joy of knowing that I was not alone.

So I prayed, and as I listened to the promptings of the Spirit, I was led to a decision that I felt was right. Then, after I made my final choice, I took the decision back to Him in prayer and received a confirmation that it was right.

Growth comes not necessarily from having many choices but from making the right choices. You can't enjoy the ice cream until you taste it, and you can't get the full experience unless you have a full scoop. God has given us the mind and the heart to make choices. He expects us to measure and weigh things out and do the best we can. When we need to make a decision, we can turn to Him for help and guidance. Through the Holy Ghost He can gently and lovingly guide us down the path that is best for us. If we listen to and follow those promptings, we will make the right choice.

As we live the commandments and become more like our Father, our choices will begin to be more in line with the choices He would make for us. Our confidence in our decisions and our ability to make better decisions will grow stronger. The paths to choose will become more clear. We will become more like Him.

I still visit that ice cream parlor often. I was there recently with my youngest daughter. Her eyes grew wide as she looked at the rows and rows of different ice cream flavors.

"Which one do you want?" I asked.

"I don't know," she replied, her eyes fixed on the sea of frozen deliciousness before her. "You love ice cream, so I'll have what you are having, 'cuz I know you're gonna pick a good one."

I smiled to myself. I had been there enough to try all the flavors, and, yes, I knew what was good. I also knew her well enough to know what she would love.

We left a few minutes later, a chocolate fudge ice cream cone in my hand, a bubble gum cone in hers. We were both happy and, oh, so satisfied.

When we struggle with our confidence and self-perception, we often feel as though we don't have many choices, that our options are limited. The truth of the matter is that the only thing that is limited is our perspective. When we gain God's Perspective, we begin to see the bounty of opportunities before us. We can go back to school, we can write a book, we can learn to sew, we can make new friends, we can develop a talent, we can reach out of our former comfort zone for a dream we never thought was possible.

Take a moment to look at yourself now. Do you feel different from when you broke open this book? Do you see yourself differently? Can you see yourself, even a little bit, through God's eyes? Do you feel more confident? Of course you do! How can you not, knowing what He knows about you? Forget what the world thinks—God knows who are and what you can be and do, and you have made the choice to trust Him.

And because of your Perspective, you have greater confidence—

and more opportunities. In fact, you might have so many options before you that you begin to feel overwhelmed. It is times like these that you can turn to your Father and ask for His recommendations: What would Thou have me do? Where would Thou have me go? What talents would Thou have me develop so that Thou can best use me?

Listen to His recommendations through the promptings of the Holy Ghost, the words of others you trust, or that feeling inside of you that peacefully yet firmly draws you toward one choice more than others. Then make a choice, and go for it! Forget about feeling self-conscious in the eyes of man—be confident in the eyes of God. "And whatsoever ye do, do it heartily, as to the Lord, and not unto men" (Colossians 3:24). Do it for yourself. Do it for Him. Have faith in yourself, because He has faith in you.

Faith: A Choice, Not a State of Mind

We have mentioned faith in this book already—the faith we have in God and the faith He has in us. Let's explore this vital principle further because choosing to have faith is perhaps one of the most important choices you will ever make.

Some people call faith a crutch for the weak-minded, and they say that to believe in something you cannot see or prove is cowardice and ignorance. The irony of their argument is that they are acting on their own "faith" that faith is a crutch. As I see it, they disregard the principle of belief based on what they believe. That logic gives me a headache.

In today's world, it is entirely possible to find "evidence" to support nearly any opinion or belief one might choose. For example, modern science has found what is believed by some to be definitive proof and validation for many theories: Evolution. The galaxy revolves around the earth. Sugar is bad for you (I'm on the fence about this one). A problem with scientific data is that they are only as accurate and understandable as the scientist who studies them. Considering the fact that scientists are all human and imperfect, with limited knowledge and perspective, it is easy to understand why their "concrete" findings change and evolve as much as the apes they claim we came from.

My intent is not to disregard science—my father is a retired chemistry professor. There have been many wonderful and amazing discoveries in the world of science, and there is a place for data and analysis. In fact, God is the Great Scientist, and everything scientific, when looked at in the proper Perspective, denotes there is a God (Alma 30:44). True science testifies of Him.

The problem comes when science is pitted against faith and claims to be the sole source of knowledge and understanding. This causes some to look down on those who dare accept a belief that cannot be tested in a lab and proven by imperfect men. Moroni taught that "faith is things which are hoped for and not seen" (Ether 12:6).

Faith is not a weakness. Faith is not a crutch. Faith is a gift of God. Faith is a choice, a decision to believe that there is a perfect Source from whom all purpose and knowledge flow. Faith in ourselves is a decision we make to believe that, despite whatever "evidence" we have accumulated from our parents, our past, or even our own shortcomings, we can be more than who we are now. We can be better. We can be happier. We can fulfill our potential.

My faith is my choice. I choose to believe that God is my Father in Heaven. I choose to believe that Jesus Christ atoned for my sins and paid a debt that I cannot comprehend. I choose to believe that the spiritual experiences I have had are real. I choose to believe that love, kindness, service, joy, obedience to commandments, and family are keys to life's purpose. I choose to be at peace even though I do not understand everything. I choose to have faith and live by it.

One day I asked my husband, "What if I'm wrong in what I believe?" He replied simply, "Then you would have spent your whole life loving others, serving others, and believing in purpose and hope and growth—how can that be bad?"

Every person alive has faith in something. The question isn't one of having faith—it is a question of what you choose to have faith in. What do you choose to believe? And how does that belief affect your choices? Does your faith lie in money? Does it lie in your job title or in material things? Does your faith lie only in what you can see and hear? If so, what of the blind or the deaf who lack the ability to see or hear? Is thunder not real because they cannot see or hear it?

On the other hand, does your faith lie in the hope that there is purpose to your pain, that families can be together forever, that God is the author of a plan so significant and eternal that it simply isn't possible for us to fully comprehend? Shall we reject truth simply because we don't fully understand it? Is that not like a first grader denying that college exists because she lacks the ability to understand the meaning, necessity, and totality of it?

Faith requires strength and commitment. It cannot be proven, yet it can be tested. It cannot be measured, yet it can be tried. It cannot be tamed, yet it can work miracles. It cannot be bought, yet it can be rewarded. It cannot be forced, yet it can be chosen. It is so simple—a choice to believe. That's all it takes. For some, it is too simple. For others, it is too difficult. For a few, it is simply unthinkable.

But for those who have Perspective and confidence, who do make the choice to believe, who admit that there are mysteries we don't understand and purposes that extend beyond this mortal life—for those people who choose faith, the burden of proof is irrelevant. It becomes a matter of the spirit and of the heart—not of science. No amount of testing or evidence can argue with a heart and soul that has allowed itself to be touched by the Spirit of God.

If someone tries to tell you your faith is wrong or your Perspective is wrong, that person is wrong. If someone tries to tell you God doesn't love you or that it is fruitless to love Him, that person is mistaken. In his letter to the Romans, Paul said, "We are more than conquerors through him that loved us. For I am persuaded, that neither death, nor life, nor angels, nor principalities, nor powers, nor things present, nor things to come, nor height, nor depth, nor any other creature, shall be able to separate us from the love of God, which is in Christ Jesus our Lord" (Romans 8:37–39).

I read that and I want to shout, "You go, Paul!" He had Perspective. He had faith, and despite his sinful past and the persecution he endured, Paul knew how God saw him and the mission God had given him—and he chose to have faith in Him and believe Him.

We are armed with Perspective. We understand we have the power to choose. We choose to have faith in God and to see ourselves and this mortal life as He does. We know that opportunities abound. We know where to go for strength and direction. We have the confidence He wants us to have—and now we are ready to put all of these into action and become what we choose to be, what He knows we can be. We feel good about ourselves. We feel empowered. We are ready to branch out confidently, to try new experiences, to accept new calls, to go where no woman has gone before!

But before you attempt to blaze a trail of glory a mile wide and do great and wonderful things, there are two very important principles to keep in mind:

You don't have to *seem* important to do important things.

It isn't just what you do but also *how* you do it that matters.

Important Things: You Don't Have to Seem Important

When I was younger and someone asked me what I wanted to be when I grew up, I would say I wanted to be famous. I wanted a name that everyone knew—like famous people I knew about. I thought if people were famous, they must be important, and if they were important, then everyone would know about them.

As I grew older—and wiser—that desire for fame faded, partly because I outgrew childish or youthful illusions about fame bringing immortality and grandeur and partly because my sense of worth now comes from an eternal source, not from my peers.

Still, on occasion I would read about a well-known figure and their accomplishments and feel a touch of envy (one of those Enemies of Perspective). Even though my desire for the accolades of man had faded, I still wanted to do important things, to be an important person—not for the fame, but for the purpose. I wanted my life to have a great purpose, and it seemed that the important stuff was most often taken care of by the important people—famous people. Then one day a story in the scriptures reminded me of a true principle.

Hundreds of years before the birth of Jesus, the Old Testament prophet Zechariah prophesied of the Savior and His triumphant entry into Jerusalem: "Rejoice greatly, O daughter of Zion; shout, O daughter of Jerusalem: behold, thy King cometh unto thee: he is just, and having salvation; lowly, and riding upon an ass, and upon a colt the foal of an ass" (Zechariah 9:9). This triumphant entry was to be a seminal time in Jesus's life. It was a sign given to the Jews to enable them to recognize their Messiah.

This seems to qualify as a very important event.

In Matthew 21, we read about the fulfillment of Zechariah's prophecy. Jesus did enter the city riding on the back of a colt (JST Matthew 21:5). A great multitude recognized Him from the prophecy given years before, and they spread robes and tree branches upon the ground before Him. They cried, "Hosanna to the Son of David: Blessed is he that cometh in the name of the Lord; Hosanna in the highest" (Matthew 21:9). A triumphant entry, indeed!

Ponder this question for a moment: How was this very important colt obtained—a colt that was prophesied of hundreds of years earlier? The New Testament simply records that Jesus "sent two of his disciples" to fetch the colt (Luke 19:29; see also Matthew 21:1; Mark 11:1). Certainly Jesus knew a prophecy was about to be fulfilled and certainly he understood the importance of this event. But the record keeper does not name the two disciples who were sent to obtain the colt! *This prophecy was fulfilled by two men whose names were not even recorded.*

Now think about that. These unnamed disciples were asked to do something by the Lord—and they did it simply because He asked them to. They may or may not have understood the magnitude of the moment, but they were His followers, and they wanted to obey Him. In doing so, these unnamed disciples fulfilled a prophecy.

I was moved by this scripture because it taught me a powerful lesson: *I do not have to be somebody "important" to do important things. I simply have to be me and do what He asks of me.*

I offer this insight for a purpose. When we are armed with Perspective, an understanding of the power of choice, and the desire and confidence to be more and do more, we understand this: We can do amazing things, and God has a great work to perform in us and through us. We recognize that these great things and this important work may not always seem great and important to us, but they are to Him.

I am grateful now that my youthful wish did not come true. My name isn't in lights, and I am not famous. However, what I am is willing—willing to try my hardest to do what is asked of me by my Savior and my Father in Heaven. Everything they ask is important to me.

I know that sometimes it is hard to remember you are doing something important when you are cleaning the toilet or doing the laundry or stuck in traffic. The greater percentage of our lives is taken up by these seemingly mundane tasks. I've never felt much like a princess when I'm donning my yellow rubber gloves after my children have thrown up, but it is most often during those small and simple moments that the Lord truly does bring to pass great things (Alma 37:6). The truth is that it often doesn't matter what you are doing as much as it matters *why* and *how*. We do what He asks us to do because we love Him and we trust Him. When those are our motives, we understand that anything He asks us to do is important to Him.

I Was Running: Attitude and Intent Matter

My husband didn't see me run until we had been married for over five years. It's true. Athletics did not come naturally to me. I was clumsy and uncoordinated, and my classmates in my high school P.E. class didn't let me forget it. After I finished the required P.E. classes, I was glad to be done with the subject. Who needed sports and exercise? (This was back in the day when my metabolism actually worked for me.)

When I moved away from home my roommate and I joined a gym. I went once.

My husband, on the other hand, loves sports and is very athletic. He loved playing football, basketball—you name it. A few years after we were married he took up running, and he encouraged me to join him. I told him it wasn't going to happen—not because I *couldn't* run, but because I *wouldn't* run. My husband was very well aware of all my strong points, and I wasn't ready to say, "Okay, watch me look like an idiot." So I didn't run, and I wasn't ever going to . . . until I got really hungry one day.

We were late for some kind of appointment, but I really needed something to eat. He agreed to stop by a store but only if I would hurry in and grab what I wanted. I knew then and there I had a choice: go hungry or run. For the first time in our marriage, my husband saw me run. And he didn't make fun of me.

After that incident I realized how silly I had been. I had allowed the teasing of a bunch of gangly adolescents ten years earlier to make me feel self-conscious. I had, in effect, given them power over me. I decided then and there that I would no longer let the opinions of others determine what I do. Because I wanted to be healthier and stronger, I began to run. A few years later I ran my first 5k race. It was a great accomplishment for me—not so much because I actually finished, which was a major physical accomplishment, but because it represented my decision to do something that was good for me even if I thought I looked silly doing it.

What you do may not be as important as why and how you do it—or don't do it.

I almost let my resolution slide one Sunday. In our chapel there are soft pews, and there are also hard folding chairs in the back for extra seating. Those chairs are often taken by latecomers. One week, my youngest daughter asked if we could sit there. She wanted to know what it felt like to sit in the hard seats. As we scooted into our soft bench, I whispered, "Next week." I didn't really think she'd remember.

The next Sunday, as we walked up the aisle toward our usual soft bench, she tugged on my dress. "Mom," she said. "You promised we could sit on the hard chairs today."

A rush of thoughts and emotions flooded my brain. First, I had forgotten all about it and was annoyed that she remembered. I didn't want to sit in the back on the hard chairs. My rear end wasn't made for that. Second, I didn't want people to think I showed up late—I had my pride. I seated her on the bench next to me and told her this was where we were going to sit. She was deflated.

The soft cush under my tush offered little comfort to my guilty conscience. I realized that I regarded the idea of what others might think of me as more important than the promise I made to my daughter. So, ten minutes into the meeting, I stood and, with my family in tow, walked down the aisle to the back of the room and sat on the hard chairs.

My daughter beamed. She thought the cold steel was awesome. I thought she was crazy. But regardless of where I sat, or what people might have thought, I had kept my promise—and I felt great ("good guilt" had served its purpose!).

Sometimes what we do is not as important as how we do it. What is our attitude, our desire, our intent? Where I sat that day wasn't important, but my intent to keep my promise was. For me, running, by itself, was important, but even more important for me was learning to run without caring how I looked.

We will be asked to do a lot of things that we will be hesitant about. Perhaps we hesitate because we think we might look stupid or we are convinced we can't do it or that we'll do it poorly. Maybe we think we won't enjoy the task (scrubbing those toilets, for example). But it isn't the glory of the task that is important to the Lord—it is the depth of our willingness to try.

Sometimes what we do is *very* important—and in those situations, how we do it matters even more. The Lord told King David that He had chosen David's son Solomon to succeed him on the throne and to build a temple. Before David gave Solomon the "pattern" of the temple that he had received "by the spirit" (1 Chronicles 28:11–12), he gave his son this sound advice: "Know thou the God of thy father, and serve him with a perfect heart and with a willing mind: for the Lord searcheth all hearts, and understandeth all the imaginations of the thoughts" (1 Chronicles 28:9). David understood that, even though the kingly stewardship Solomon was given was important, Solomon's attitude and intent were crucial to his success. He told his son, "If thou seek [the Lord], he will be found of thee." David knew that how Solomon carried out his task was every bit as important as the task itself.

We need to trust in the Lord and give Him our all. I have learned that I must lay my fear and my issues on the altar before Him, and in exchange I will receive the confidence that can come only from Him. David was telling Solomon that he needed to align the desires and attitudes of his heart and mind with God's. David understood that what you focus on is where you will end up, and he wanted Solomon to be close to God.

After David made sure Solomon understood the importance of how he should conduct himself as king—with a perfect heart and a willing mind—he then said, "Take heed now; for the Lord hath chosen thee to build an house for the sanctuary: be strong and do it" (1 Chronicles 28:10).

Be strong and do it. What powerful words!

This advice applies as much to us in our stewardships as it did to Solomon in his. God will ask us to do many things in our lives— some things that might seem difficult or even impossible for us to do. It is up to us to decide if—and how—we will do them.

Paul taught the Corinthians: "For if there be first a willing mind, it is accepted according to that a man hath, and not according to that he hath not" (2 Corinthians 8:12). God knows we will not do everything perfectly. We "have not" that capacity. God asks for a willing mind and an honest effort, and He will take care of the rest in His own way.

An understanding of these two principles—"You don't have to seem important to do important things" and "It isn't just what you do but how you do it that matters"—frees us from self-imposed expectations of what things are important, how perfectly we need to do them, and how we should look doing them.

Some of the things God wants us to accomplish may not seem

important in the world's eyes, and many of them we may not feel we are doing well. I believe that God would like us to stop wasting time and opportunities because we harbor fear and false expectations. Be willing to do what He asks. Be willing to discover new talents and skills. Be willing to look stupid once in a while. Just be *willing*—then be strong and do it!

Who Do You Want To Be? Take Control and Choose

I believe that God is pleased when we think and ponder and dream. He wants us to consider our possibilities, to want to be better. He wants us to discover our talents and develop them. As we do that, we are able to serve Him in new ways. We find joy in being an instrument in His hands and in discovering who we are and deciding, with His help, who we want to be.

One of the greatest gifts God has given us, next to agency and akin to it, is the right and opportunity to improve and progress. In all aspects of our lives, we are constantly changing. The changes may be momentous and life-altering or so minute they are nearly imperceptible, but change is our constant companion.

When we go to bed at night, we are not the same person we were when we awoke that morning. Our faith is stronger or weaker than it was in the morning, and so is our level of happiness and satisfaction, our commitment to God and family, our level of talent and ability, and so forth. For better or for worse, we change every day.

This gift of opportunity to change puts the power in our hands to control who we are, who we will become, where we go, where we end up, and how happy we are along the way.

When we ponder the Atonement of Jesus Christ, our minds might turn to the repentance and forgiveness that it affords. But the Atonement reaches even beyond forgiveness—it brings power to

126

change for the better. When we apply the Atonement in our lives, we are upgraded from solo-participant in mortality to being a partner with God. As we humbly acknowledge our nothingness, we can begin to tap into our greatness.

A beautiful thing about the Atonement is that we don't have to wait for its power to take effect in our lives. One of my favorite verses in all scripture testifies that when we "come forth" and prepare our hearts, "*immediately* shall the great plan of redemption be brought about unto you" (Alma 34:31; emphasis added). This gives me such a feeling of hope! As we rid ourselves of the Enemies of Perspective and turn to God, immediately the power of the Atonement of Jesus Christ can begin to change us for the better.

This empowering truth touches every aspect of our lives and not only those that we might categorize as spiritual. Anything that we desire—and work for—that is righteous and is for our benefit the Lord will help us achieve and attain.

I've never been the "outdoorsy" type. I enjoyed camping to a point—when I wasn't afraid of the bears. But I wasn't a hiker or a swimmer or anything like that. I didn't even like granola bars. That just wasn't me.

What does that have to do with the Atonement, agency, and change? Everything.

One day I was thinking about what is and isn't "me." In the past I had considered my likes and dislikes and had mentally labeled myself as one who didn't like being outdoors, that I "didn't do dirt." At the time it seemed a logical acknowledgment of who I was. But I realized later that this wasn't just a harmless observation of my personality type; it was a declaration and, in a way, a condemnation. I had told myself that I was not an outdoorsy person, so I never pursued an interest in the outdoors. Then I came to realize that whenever you say, "I don't do [fill in the blank]," you never will.

Because I don't like the thought of limiting myself, I decided that I actually did want to be "outdoorsy." I started running outside for exercise rather than on the treadmill. I started bicycling, as well. I realized that I enjoyed being outside. The fresh air smelled and felt good. *I* felt good.

There was a trail near my home where I occasionally ran or rode. The trail ran beside a river and over an old train trestle. On one of my first "outdoorsy" rides, I stopped at a bend in the river and took a picture.

A cool breeze kissed my tired cheeks as the smell of the river and the pine trees filled my nose. The sound of the rushing water, accompanied by songs of the birds, stirred something inside me, as though a little part of me was changing. Like the way the Velveteen Rabbit turned from a stuffed bunny to a real rabbit, I started to feel as though I was turning into a "real" outdoor person—and I liked it.

Was it the Atonement that turned me into a lover of the outdoors? Did it change part of who I was? I believe it did. Through the power of the Atonement of Jesus Christ, we may choose the paths we take and the people we want to be. We have the power to direct our lives and to progress and grow. We are damned only by sin, not by personality type, geographic factors, or even social factors. It was with that power that I decided I wanted to be something different than I thought I was. Through my own choices and efforts, I gained experience and was given the gift of change.

Think of who you are right now. Is it who you want to be? Have you labeled yourself a certain way? Are there things you "don't do"? Are there things you would like to try, different habits or strengths you would like to develop? You can. If they are righteous and good desires, God will help you become who you want to be. I know that He hopes you will.

If you don't "do crafts," you can decide you want to become a crafty person. Find someone who is good at it and learn. If you aren't "outdoorsy," you can decide you want to become so and do it. You can become good at math, you can be more patient, a better speaker, less afraid, a better singer, a stronger athlete—whatever it is you want to be. The first step is recognizing that you have the power to let the labels go and choose for yourself who and what you will become.

Of course, there is no guarantee that if you want to be rich you will be a millionaire or that if you want to be a singer you will win *American Idol* or that if you want to run in a 5k you won't look silly—but you will never know until you make that choice and try.

Every day we change for the better—or for the worse. Take control. Who will you be today? Who do you want to be tomorrow? Take a moment and write down some ideas, some dreams you've had, some goals you might have given up on. If they are good and righteous desires, seek after them. Take them to the Lord and ask Him to help. You have gifts you have kept hidden and gifts you are not yet aware of. Have the courage to seek them out. Have the faith to be who you want to be—whatever that is. Know that with the help of Heavenly Father and Jesus Christ, you can do more and be better than you ever could on your own.

Better: With God by Our Side

I've sung in my church choir for years. I love to sing. I am not a great singer—I'm probably not even very good—but I put my heart into it, and I love to do it. Our choir director is wonderful. She has never told me how poorly I sing, even when I ask her directly. She always says the same thing: "You have a beautiful voice." I love her for that. Over the years she has given great counsel and direction to the choir, and because we have followed it, we have all improved, but I am still far from where I want to be.

A few years ago, a woman named Marianne joined our choir. She was young and adorable, and, oh, so talented. She sat three seats away from me during her first practice. I could hear her beautiful voice drift to my ears. Oh, how I wished I could sing like that! A few weeks later, Marianne sat next to me during choir practice. As the choir began to sing, I found myself feeling a bit envious of her. Why couldn't Heavenly Father have given me that kind of voice? He knew how much I loved to sing. He also knew how sad it made me feel when I felt the music so strongly in my heart but my voice couldn't get it out. I sat next to Marianne that day, half-singing and half-sulking.

But then, as we continued to practice, I noticed that something was happening. Without realizing it, I had begun to sing better. My tone was richer, my voice was clearer, and my notes did not go sharp as often. It was a small miracle! I could sing better, and I was ecstatic! I sang in the shower all week (because that is where I do my best singing). Then Sunday came again, and it was time for choir practice. We sang the same songs we had been practicing for the past few weeks, the same songs that I had sung so well the week before. But this time was different: I sounded terrible again! I cleared my throat and tried harder. Still bad. What happened to the miracle from the week before? I heard Marianne's voice from three chairs over and I realized something: She was a better singer than I, but when I was next to her, singing by her side, I was better than when I was alone. *I was a better singer when I was with her.*

On the way home, I thought about that experience and how it illustrated an eternal truth. In Joshua 1, we read the account of Joshua, the man who was called to succeed Moses in leading the Israelites. Their prophet and leader was gone, and now, after forty years of wandering, it was up to Joshua to lead them in a battle with Canaan to reclaim their promised land.

If I were in Joshua's position, I would have been terrified. The

Lord knew how Joshua was feeling, and He gave him a beautiful pep talk: "I will be with thee; I will not fail thee, nor forsake thee. Be strong and of a good courage" (Joshua 1:5–6).

The Lord told Joshua that he would be able to rise to the occasion because the Lord would be by his side: "Be not afraid, neither be thou dismayed; for the Lord thy God is with thee whithersoever thou goest" (Joshua 1:9). Joshua believed the Lord and went on to fight many battles, braver, stronger, and a better leader than he could have been on his own.

As I mentioned before, Paul also felt the empowerment that comes from being in the Lord's company. "I can do all things through Christ which strengtheneth me," he said (Philippians 4:13). Ammon shared the same passion: "I know that I am nothing; as to my strength I am weak; therefore I will not boast of myself, but I will boast of my God, for in his strength I can do all things" (Alma 26:12). Our relationship with—and our spiritual proximity to—Heavenly Father and Jesus Christ can make us better people than we are when we are alone. I can teach my children better, I can see my purpose better, I can endure trials better, I can live better, I can love better, I can forgive better, I can be better with Them by my side.

How wonderful is this principle of personal magnification: No matter what comes up in choir practice, I know I can sing better with Marianne at my side. No matter what comes up in life, as I exercise my faith and stay close to my Father in Heaven and my Savior, I know I can be better than the person I am now—I can become as They intend me to be. I can be me—but better.

Go and Do: The Armor of Confidence

In a letter to the Ephesians, Paul admonished them to put on "the whole armour of God" (Ephesians 6:10–18). He spoke about the breastplate of righteousness, the shield of faith, and so forth. It is beautiful imagery, and I will borrow that imagery to present to you what I call the Whole Armor of Confidence:

"Finally, my sisters, be strong in the Lord, and in the power of His might.

"Put on the whole Armor of Confidence, that ye may be able to stand against the wiles of the devil.

"For we wrestle not against flesh and doughnuts, but against principalities, against powers, against the rulers of the darkness of this world, against spiritual and emotional misperceptions in personal places.

"Wherefore, take unto you the whole Armor of Confidence, that ye may be able to withstand in the evil day of trying on swimsuits, and having done all, to stand, feeling beautiful.

"Stand therefore, having your loins girt about with truth, and having the breastplate of courage and hope;

"And your feet shod with the knowledge of who you are;

"Above all, taking the shield of faith and Perspective, wherewith ye shall be able to quench the fiery darts of the wicked and the media and the Enemies of Perspective.

"And take the helmet of knowledge, and the sword of agency, which is your power to choose;

"Praying always with all prayer and supplication in the Spirit, and watching thereunto with all perseverance and supplication for your purpose."

When we have put on our Armor of Confidence, we are ready to "go and do," to "fight the good fight." I know that's what the Lord expects of us—to have confidence in ourselves and in Him and to move forward in that confidence.

A story about two missionaries was shared with me. They had planned to go tracting. The first missionary was eager to start knocking on doors, but the second had a different idea. For quite some time, he stood, with his eyes closed and without moving, in the middle of the house-lined street. Finally, the first missionary asked him what he was doing.

"I'm tracting," he said. "I stand in the middle of the road and pray until I feel impressed to go to a certain house."

Of course, God has the power to tell them exactly which house they should approach, but usually that is not the way He works. Missionary work requires effort and obedience. There is a purpose for knocking on all kinds of doors as the Lord's servants search for the people He has prepared for them to teach.

It is the same for us in our daily lives. God could easily tell us what steps to take—and sometimes He does. But usually we learn by searching out all kinds of opportunities and options. As we do this prayerfully, we are led to where He wants us to be. I believe that *we cannot be led unless we are moving.*

The Lord has told us that we need to be actively "engaged in a good cause" (D&C 58:27), having a strong desire to serve Him and to show our love for Him through our choices. This life is His gift to us. What we do with it is our gift to Him.

I believe He is pleased when we hope, choose, and *do*. I don't think He is pleased with fence-sitters. He said, "I know thy works, that thou art neither cold nor hot: I would thou wert cold or hot. So then because thou art lukewarm, and neither cold nor hot, I will spue thee out of my mouth" (Revelation 3:15–16). These words may seem harsh, but they are from the Lord Himself.

I'm convinced that He doesn't want us to wait or to be lukewarm in our love for and confidence in ourselves and Him. He doesn't want us to stand in the middle of the road, wearing our Armor of Confidence, and wait for Him to tell us exactly where to go. He wants us to get up and go, to move and get busy. He has prepared people to help us, people for us to help, opportunities to learn and grow, experiences that will lead to joy and peace. He wants us to start knocking on the doors that will lead us to where He wants us to be.

James admonished, "Be ye *doers* of the word, and not hearers only" (James 1:22; emphasis added).

You have been given gifts and talents for a reason. As you grow and discover what you can do, the scope of your mind and spirit will be enlarged. You will evolve from an insecure, one-task tool into a confident, multifaceted tool He can use for many purposes in many situations. God needs confident women who are willing to say, "I can do that, and if I can't, I'm still willing to try my hardest."

As you exercise more faith in yourself and in Him, you will be amazed at the things He will accomplish in you and through you. You will find the power He has given you to choose your own path, to own your own life—*if* you believe. We must not be like the people Jesus found in "his own country": "He could there do no mighty work . . . because of their unbelief" (Mark 6:4–6).

It is not enough to simply believe—we must *do*. You may not need to start running, ride your bike on a trail, or sit on the hard chairs at church. But you must *do* something, for it is in the *doing* that the *seeing* and *choosing* are realized.

Remember: Who you are now is God's gift to you. Who you become is your gift to Him.

What will your gift be?

Chapter Six

She Shoots! She Scores! . . . not

The Pearls of Progress

*He who cherishes a beautiful vision, a lofty ideal
in his heart, will one day realize it.*
James Allen

Let me tell you about the time I broke a woman's nose. It's a great story—but I'm getting ahead of myself . . .

Now that we have donned our Armor of Confidence and understand the power of choosing, we are excited and ready for the doing, for the progress and opportunities that lie before us. But progress itself can bring new problems, thoughts, or doubts that we need to be aware of. These are the "Phase 2" tactics that the adversary uses when he sees we are making progress in our confident quest. He will do all he can to stop us from progressing, to have us become lukewarm in our beliefs, confidence, and effort.

In this chapter we discuss the Pearls of Progress—principles that can help us succeed in our quest. The better we understand the Pearls of Progress, the greater chance we have of staying on the path that we—and our Heavenly Father—know will bring us the greatest joy.

She Shoots! She Scores! . . . Not:
You Just Have to Be Willing

In chapter 5, I mentioned that I had decided not to let the opinions of others dictate what I do—and I meant it. I held fast to that creed—until a friend asked me to join our women's basketball team at church.

I didn't like basketball. I didn't understand it. I wasn't good at it. I wasn't coordinated. I knew from past experience that not only was I awful at it but I looked absolutely ridiculous playing it. So I said no, I wouldn't do it.

My friend asked again. I said no again.

She asked again. I said no again.

Then she didn't ask me again.

That is when I really thought about it—not about what they were asking me to do but about why I didn't want to do it. I realized this very clear truth about myself: I don't like to do in public things that I am not good at. I don't like to look stupid, and I knew if I said yes to being on the team, I would look stupid. Then I had another realization: this was the same issue that in the past had kept me from running. I was afraid of what others would think; I was afraid of looking stupid.

After even further introspection, I recognized that because of this fear, I had never given sports a real try. I had always figured I could blame my awkwardness on my ignorance or lack of practice. I realized that there was a chance—albeit a small one—that I might actually be good at basketball if I really tried.

So I called my friend and said I'd join.

You've heard people say that all your dreams will come true if you just want them bad enough. It's not true. I went to every practice and even stayed afterward for one-on-one coaching from my friend.

I studied the rules of basketball and watched games on TV. I really tried my hardest—and I was still awful. I was so bad that during the games no one was assigned to guard me. In fact, when I got the ball, I'm pretty sure I saw the other team take a power nap.

I was my own worst enemy. Picture a hunched-over, middle-aged woman jumping on hot coals with a slippery ball in her hands. That was me. I know because I asked my husband to videotape a game so I could watch myself and improve my "technique." We were told during practice that we should never stop moving, so I didn't! I moved constantly. Even when I didn't have the ball I did a strange tapping-hopping thing with my arms outstretched, ready for a ball that was rarely passed my way. And when I did get the ball, it was still a sad sight to behold. I would fling it into the air with a jerky kind of body push, and invariably I would miss. She shoots! She scores! . . . Not!

It was truly sad to watch.

But I did it. Even though I had sure knowledge that I looked totally inept, I still gave my best effort in every game—and it was liberating! I learned that I could look clueless and I would still be okay. I also learned that with a positive attitude, full-on enthusiasm, and total commitment, I would still be terrible at playing basketball, and that was okay, too. The point is, I threw my fear of looking stupid and not being good at something out the window and tried my hardest. And that felt great!

With each game my confidence grew—not confidence in my ability, but confidence in giving my unadulterated effort. To my great satisfaction, I began to foul other players (I was told that you know you're playing hard when you foul someone). Toward the end of the season, I even made a basket!

I have to give props to my friend and basketball mentor. From the first time I rejected her invitation, through the clumsy practices and my granny-esque game performance, she never once said that I was as awful as I knew I was. My self-disparaging remarks were always met with "You weren't that bad" or "You should feel good—you've really improved." I really was "that bad," but she had a gift for seeing my potential, as small as it was, and focusing on the positive. She often complimented me on any progress I made, such as the time I shot a free throw that hit the backboard rather than flying past it. In a recent conversation about those church basketball games, I said to her, "Do you remember how bad I was?" Without missing a beat, she responded, "I remember our games, and you weren't bad at all." When she said that, my love for her grew two sizes because I really was that bad, and she really is that good. I have always loved her for the kindness, patience, and confidence she showed me.

Despite my lack of athletic prowess, playing basketball was a positive experience, although I can't really say it was fun. My joy came not from playing ball but from giving it my all. For me, that was enough.

Until *she* came along.

She was serious about sports. She was confident, athletic, and really good. She was my friend's older sister, and she wanted to win. I found myself a bit frightened and highly intimidated by her. But I was still determined to play my hardest, even though I knew I'd get pummeled. The first time we played against her team, we lost by a landslide, but by the end of the game I didn't care. I was just glad it was over.

A few weeks later, we were scheduled to play her team again. I was feeling a little more confident by then, and I told myself I would be fine—until during the game I saw her running toward me. *Not her. Anyone but her!* I did what any talented ballplayer would do: I closed my eyes and prayed that she would disappear.

A scream pulled my attention back to the game, and I opened my eyes to see her lying on the floor with her hand over her bloody face. While I was fervently praying, someone had run into her and accidentally smacked her right in the nose. Her nose was broken. She was out the rest of the season.

I admit it. I was relieved she was gone, although I felt awful for the way it happened, and for a long time after, I felt guilty for praying that she would "disappear." (Later, I learned it wasn't my prayer but *her own sister* who had laid her low!)

This story is not about receiving answers to prayer. I am certain that her nose was not broken for my sake. The real point of the story is this: God knows we are not going to be good at everything. I'm sure He doesn't require us to be the best homemaker, speaker, teacher, chef, and so forth. What He does ask is that we do our best in action and in attitude—that we have a willing heart.

I don't think it was important to God that I played basketball well. I'm glad for that, because I didn't play well, despite my honest best efforts. I have never shed a tear because I am a bad basketball player. That doesn't matter. What mattered was my attitude.

It's okay not to be good at everything. I can't multitask in the kitchen. I burn things when I try to multitask. I accept my limitations and operate within the boundaries that work for me. (For example, I stare at the oven timer and eat cookie dough while the cookies are baking so I won't forget they are in the oven. It's a sacrifice I am willing to make.)

Don't let the fear (or knowledge) that you won't be good at something hold you back. Go and do with faith and joy in the trying, and you'll be amazed at what you can accomplish.

Jump Already: Trust God and Move Forward

I have always liked to consider myself a brave person, a fearless and adventurous one who dreams of skydiving and other daring things. Notice I didn't say I actually am a brave person—I said I like to "consider" myself a brave person. But reality? That's a different story. A few years ago my family went to the northern California Sierra foothills to swim and have fun with some good friends. The landscape was beautiful. We were surrounded by a jagged, clay-colored wall of rock that towered above the river on one side and a wall of bushy trees and plants on the other. The contrasting natural walls created a pool in one part of the river. We swam and played and enjoyed each other's company.

It wasn't too long before the boys found a way to climb up the rock wall and take turns jumping into the river. The more adventurous ones found an even higher place to climb up to and jump off from. They whooped and hollered as they leaped off the small ledges into the deep water, over and over. They made it look fun and easy.

Late in the afternoon, because I was a "brave person," I pridefully dared myself to climb up to the higher ledge and jump off. I was excited to make the leap, to feel the exhilarating rush of air that drove other jumpers—including my five-year-old son—to yell, "Woohoo!" as they plummeted toward the cool water. As I climbed higher and higher, I visualized myself reaching the ledge, standing tall, and bravely dropping into the water, emerging triumphant and overjoyed.

The rocks were slippery from the wet feet of previous brave jumpers, making for a difficult ascent. When I finally reached the higher ledge, I brushed some dirt from my knees and stood up to take in the view. The trees were beautiful, the water serene, and the people so . . . small!

Suddenly, my body froze as my mind kicked into hyperspeed. How far up was I? What had I been thinking? It didn't take me long to realize I was faced with two options: leap to my death or climb down. The latter seemed to be the more responsible route.

I turned to make my way back down to safety, but my own ascent to the ledge had made the rocks even muddier and more slippery. It took only a few steps to realize it would be nearly impossible to climb down without certain injury. I slowly turned around. In a moment of fear and defeat, I faced the terrifying truth: There was only one way down—to jump.

You might think that having only one escape route would expedite my decision to actually make the leap, but it didn't. Forget all the "brave" mumbo-jumbo. When it got right down to it, I was scared.

My family and friends tried to encourage me: "You can do it!" they shouted. "It'll be fun!" But their encouraging words had no power over me. I was stuck. After thirty minutes of standing on the ledge, I heard the tenor of their words change: "Come on, even your son did it, and he's only five!" Their patience was growing thin, but I still could not bring myself to jump. I just wasn't ready to die.

When you look at a situation through the eyes of fear, you are not seeing it as it really is. My initial vision of an adventurous, fun jump into the water had now become an inevitable dive to a painful death. The ledge had, in my eyes, become a great cliff that was surely starting to crumble. The surface of the water took on the appearance of glass— glass that I just knew concealed dozens of sharp rocks underneath.

I couldn't trust my own eyes, so I made my husband splash the water to prove that it wasn't, indeed, made of glass. I even made him dive down to the bottom to prove there were no rocks. Still, I could not jump. An hour passed, and I was getting cold. My family and friends had lost their patience. The sun was going down, and it was time to leave. They were ready to go, but I still didn't want to die.

Finally, after over an hour of encouraging me, splashing the water, and diving to the bottom of the pool, my husband looked up to me and simply said, "You are right. You can't do it. It's too hard. It's time to go. I'll come up and help you down the rock path."

He said the magic words: "You can't do it. It's too hard." Now, I don't like to be told what I can and can't do. I admit that part of that is pride. But the other part is simple: I like to do hard things. I like to push myself to do the best job possible. I don't like limitations. I find it very ironic that most of the limitations we experience are ones we put on ourselves. My husband's "loving" statement brought me back to that realization.

I looked at him and simply said, "Yes, I can." Then I jumped.

The moments after my feet left the cliff were thrilling! I felt the wind rush past my ears. I felt my stomach come into my throat. I closed my eyes and screamed out of sheer excitement—and slight terror. Then I splashed into the water—there were no glass or rocks, just cool, safe water! As I emerged from the river, I was filled with joy for two reasons: One, I had done it and I was alive! And two, I knew I would never have to do it ever again. I was triumphant!

Because of the hour of doubt and fear that preceded my jump, some people might discount the triumphant outcome, but I don't. I learned that day that *the true test of courage and bravery is not in being unafraid but in doing what you know you should do—and could do— even when you are afraid.*

My experience wasn't a battle between good and evil, and the outcome did not affect my eternal salvation, but it does have application to the rest of our lives: We can do hard things, we can do scary things, even when we are afraid.

Sometimes in life we feel like we are making progress. We're trying hard, we're growing, and we're climbing. Then one day, we find ourselves standing on a ledge—emotionally, intellectually, or spiritually—as we face a difficult trial or circumstance or a new experience or opportunity. We have people to help us. Our Father in Heaven knows we can do it—He's promised we will not be given more than we can handle, even though at times we might doubt our own capacity.

At those times it is good to remember that other simple truth: Many of our limitations are those we put on ourselves because of fear and doubt. Think about it. Have you ever not pursued the perfect job because you deemed yourself to be unqualified? Have you passed up a possible relationship because you didn't want to get hurt? Have you hesitated to give help because you assumed you had nothing to offer? How many good and right opportunities do we pass up because we are afraid or don't think we are capable?

Life is difficult and full of challenges. That is the plan. If it were easy, where would the victory be? But life is also filled with great opportunities and grand adventures that require faith and courage. Many of the things we can and should do will be hard. We need to prove to ourselves that we can do hard things and not limit ourselves because of self-doubt, fear, or despair. We need to jump.

When we are standing on the precipice of something scary, we need to recognize the Enemies of Perspective and cast them out. We need to be "inspired by a better cause" (Alma 43:45). Sometimes the only way to get where you need to be is to trust the Lord and then jump in with both feet. He will be there when we land, and He has promised that we will land safely.

I still remember the feeling of those few seconds between the ledge and the water. I prayed, I was scared, I screamed, I flew! I did it. And it was worth it.

Pass Me Another Cookie: Moderation Is a Key to Success

Everywhere I turn these days I hear a skinny person saying, "Cookies are bad for you." Frankly, I get tired of hearing it. I like cookies—no, I love cookies.

If you don't believe me, you should see what is written by my doorbell: "No soliciting—unless you're selling cookies. Seriously, we really like cookies."

As I've gotten older, though, I have learned something very important about cookies: Too much of a good thing can be bad. Here are some lessons I've learned from solid personal experience:

1. If you eat a dozen Oreos with two cups of milk before bed, you have strange or disturbing dreams.

2. If, during the day, you eat a chocolate chip cookie every time you walk by the cookie jar, your kids will be disappointed when they come home and find an empty cookie jar.

3. When you eat five snickerdoodles in one sitting, one of them is used as energy, and, unfortunately, the other four find permanent housing in your thighs.

4. If you inhale a dozen Christmas sugar cookies before dinner, there won't be any room in your stomach for vegetables.

Eating cookies in moderation isn't bad. Eating cookies by the dozen is bad. In fact, too much of anything—even good things—can be bad for you.

Life is filled with demands—demands on our time, our energy, our minds, and our souls. It is hard to juggle everything that is expected of us by others and especially by ourselves. We can get caught up in trying to keep our house spotless, taking our kids to all kinds of lessons and sports, serving a healthy dinner every night, studying our scriptures, serving others—and don't forget exercising and showering every day, which is tough when you've got a gaggle of young children! We try to do everything, all at once, every day. We do too much. We are too busy, and we become frazzled.

We end up feeling we've disappointed someone or that we have failed somehow. We are unable to appreciate the fruits of our labors, and we feel under par. So we try to squeeze more into each day—each minute—until we find there is no room for other, perhaps better, things or even room to breathe.

I have been learning to love one of my husband's favorite words: *moderation*. It's a principle of balance and temperance. It's a principle that I struggle with. My ideal is to be the best mother and wife I can be, so I put together a list of things I think a perfect mother and wife would do: Get up with my children every morning and share a prepared spiritual message, kneel for family prayer twice a day, never holler at my kids, volunteer in their classrooms once a week, join the PTA, read to them an hour a day, have dinner on the table at six o'clock every night, play games and take walks with them, make sure they are getting good grades and that they are involved in sports and music . . . Ouch, my brain is getting tired. I have made similar lists regarding work, school, my figure, my service in church, my spiritual well-being, my service to the community, and so forth. The lists are simply too long, and, frankly, they are exhausting and terribly unrealistic.

Sometimes I can't help myself—with me, it's "go big or go home." My husband tries to help. He tells me that when we go out for ice cream I don't need to get the double scoop in a waffle cone every time; a single scoop is sufficient. But for me, moderation seems like deprivation—it's only for losers who can't have it all or do it all.

In reality, of course, moderation is not deprivation or desperation. It's inspiration. We could say that God teaches us in "moderation"—He gives us instruction line upon line, precept upon precept. He doesn't drop everything on us at once because He knows it would be too much for us to handle. He usually gives us trials in moderation, too, although it may not always feel that way. I believe that God uses the principle of moderation, and He wants us to learn about and apply it in our lives. There are many things we *want* to do that we *can* do—especially if we are wearing our Armor of Confidence—but we need to know where to draw the line.

A concept that is corollary to the principle of moderation is the ability to distinguish between choices that are good, better, and best. We can become exhausted trying to be good, or even better, at everything we do. We might have success in some areas, but it may be wiser, and more in line with God's will for us, to learn what is best for us to focus on and become the "best" at doing that particular thing. Every person has his or her own "best" thing to focus on. There is no "one size" that fits "all" of us.

Elder Dallin H. Oaks encouraged families not to become "over-scheduled." Regarding the daunting task of figuring out how to spend our time, Elder Oaks said, "As we consider various choices, we should remember that it is not enough that something is good. Other choices are better, and still others are best. Even though a particular choice is more costly, its far greater value may make it the best choice of all" ("Good, Better, Best," 104–5).

Who should determine what and how much we need to do?

I believe you are an intelligent reader. Take a look at your life and see what you observe. Are you missing spending time in the evenings with your children (perhaps the best choice) because you are busy working on PTA responsibilities (a good choice)? Are you failing to feast upon the scriptures (a best choice) because you are sleeping in (maybe a good choice)? You get the picture. Take a look at where you are spending your time. You may need to let some "good" things go to make room for "better" things. You may need to scale back on some of the better things to make room for the best things. You'll know what they are.

Inspiration leads to moderation. Pray. Ask your Father in Heaven for guidance. Think about what is most important in your life and allow Him to help you prioritize your list. Then start at the bottom and begin cutting. For example, for me, this means I have never joined the PTA. I know many amazing mothers who have, and I applaud them. Maybe that is one of the "best" things they can do for themselves and their kids. And maybe it would be a "good" thing for me, but I know it's not the *best* thing for me to do right now.

When we think about the adversary and his tactics, we often focus on the negative things he whispers directly to us, and we overlook his not-so-obvious practice of using distraction. One of his sneakiest weapons is to get us to replace the best priorities with good ones, to try to lure us away from things that matter most. He doesn't seem to care whether you are doing terrible things or good things as long as he can keep you from doing the *best* things you can do—the things that God would have you do.

A good priority is not as good when it keeps you from the best priorities. A "weed" is often a flower that has grown where it is unwanted. Good things in our lives can become weeds if they keep us from doing what is best.

Perhaps this means cutting out your kids' third sports club or turning the TV off at 9:00 p.m. rather than zoning out until midnight and being tired the next morning. Maybe it means exercising twenty minutes a day instead of a full hour. Maybe it means serving macaroni and cheese once a week instead of trying to make fresh homemade meals every night. I can't tell you what your list should include. You need to pray and figure it out with the guidance of your Father in Heaven.

Remember the sisters, Mary and Martha, in the book of Luke? I have always been a "Martha" kind of person. When I have guests, I'm the one who makes sure all their needs are met, the food is good, and everything is cleaned up (but I still don't have those cute mason jars to drink out of). To be honest, I used to be kind of upset that Mary did not help Martha more.

We read in Luke 10 that Jesus and possibly several other people were visiting the sisters' home. Martha was working hard to be a good hostess and was probably becoming stressed and frustrated because Mary wasn't helping her. Finally, Martha said to Jesus, "Lord, dost thou not care that my sister hath left me to serve alone?" (Luke 10:40).

It is interesting to note that Martha seemed to associate Jesus' care for her with the level of His awareness and concern. It probably wasn't a large house, and He apparently could see that she was "cumbered about much serving." Why didn't He ask Mary to help her? Didn't He care?

Jesus did love Martha, and He knew her well. "Martha, Martha," He said, repeating her name sweetly and tenderly. "Thou art careful and troubled about many things: but one thing is needful: and Mary hath chosen that good part, which shall not be taken away from her" (Luke 10:42).

This kind answer shows Jesus' love for Martha as He tried to teach her that, although there are good things to focus on, learning His word is a better—even the best—thing. He loved her so much that He wanted what was best for her; He wanted her to hear His word.

Many of the things that trouble us are things that will not last—a spotless house, the latest fashion, a thin figure, and so forth. We sometimes allow these things to take us away from the things that God would have us hear and do.

It can be a struggle to learn to do things in moderation. I still love cookies, and I can eat a whole box in one sitting if I am not careful. And every day I feel pulled in many directions—there are so many needs to fill. Some days I understand how Bilbo Baggins felt when he said, "I feel all thin, sort of *stretched*, if you know what I mean: like butter that has been scraped over too much bread" (Tolkien, *Fellowship*, 32).

I often feel stretched too thin, but I'm trying. I go on—one scoop at a time, one cookie at a time, and one choice at a time—and try to do the few *best* things the *best* I can. It makes sense. It's a better way to live. The guilt, the pressure, and the stress have decreased. My relationships with my Heavenly Father, my family, and myself have grown stronger. I'm learning to trust my Heavenly Father when He tells me that He will make up for all the things I simply cannot do right now. Honestly, it is so much easier than trying to do everything all the time.

One thing to keep in mind is that your good, better, and best choices may be different at different times in your life. Make it a habit to regularly review what and how you're doing. Are you scaling back on the good and the better? Or have the best things begun to take a backseat to the good and the better? If so, get out the scissors and start cutting.

Ouch, I Slipped: Keep Your Eye on the Prize

When I was ten, I was the best climber in our cul-de-sac. What I lacked in coordination, I made up for in climbing prowess. I could climb to the top of the streetlight, barefoot, and back down again while holding my breath. I could climb swingsets in the backyard and the soccer goalposts at my school.

One of my favorite things was to climb up on my neighbor's split-rail fence and balance along the top. It was a bear of a fence. The horizontal beams were wedge-shaped, with rounded bottoms and sides that sloped up to a sharp point at the top. The ends were shaped like a piece of pie or pizza.

Many a child had tried to balance on that sharp pointed edge and had fallen off. But I could balance on it and make my way ever so carefully, yet, oh, so gracefully to the other end. I imagined I was a ballerina or a tightrope performer—a favorite with my young neighborhood fans.

One hot California summer afternoon, I climbed on the fence

and stood at one end, ready for another great performance. With confidence, I began parading to the other end, twenty feet away. I had done this many times. I didn't even need to look at my feet anymore. I closed my eyes for effect. "Oooh! Aaaah!"—the crowd, consisting of five neighbor kids from age three to age nine and my four brothers, loved it. With my eyes closed and my thoughts focused on how well I was doing, I didn't notice the hints of a growing breeze.

In an instant, I felt an unseasonal rush of wind, and I slipped—but not off the fence. My feet slipped, one to each side, straddling the beam. I landed with full force onto the pointed top side of the wedge-shaped log. I thought I would die from the pain and the humiliation. How could I have been so stupid? If only I had kept my eyes open. I hobbled inside, and my mom nursed my wounded body and my bruised ego.

Looking back, of course, I see how it happened. I was overly confident. I was so sure of my ability that I no longer felt the need for constant care and caution. I had grown complacent in my performance. I closed my eyes—and I slipped.

Sometimes in my life I feel that I am doing great. Things are going well, I'm doing things right, and I feel like I've got things down. Then I close my spiritual eyes, and I slip. I do something I shouldn't do, I make a bad choice, I say a bad thing, or I give in to temptation.

Like balancing on the pointed fence, balancing a spiritual existence in a physical world can be difficult. Sometimes we do better than at other times. We become secure in our current level of growth and think, "All is well." Our sense of security may be followed by complacency and then carelessness.

Paul warned about this: "Wherefore let him that thinketh he standeth take heed lest he fall" (1 Corinthians 10:12). We must be ever vigilant and aware of our standing before God and our efforts to stay where He would have us be.

Parents have always warned, "Keep your eyes open!" I think our Heavenly Father says the same thing. The scriptures are full of admonitions to "watch"—to keep our eyes open:

"Watch ye therefore, and pray always" (Luke 21:36).

"Watch ye, stand fast in the faith" (1 Corinthians 16:13).

"See that ye are not lifted up unto pride; yea, see that ye do not boast in your own wisdom, nor of your much strength" (Alma 38:11).

With our eyes open, we can focus on our goals as we purposefully and humbly take each step. We can be aware of our surroundings and shift our balance and focus to compensate for our challenges. We can be confident in our abilities, and, with hopeful and cheerful diligence, we can keep complacency at bay and reach our goals.

Of course, we still might fall once in a while. That's okay. That is why we have been given the gift of the Atonement. Wounds are made to heal, and so are we. The important thing is to "press toward the mark for the prize" (Philippians 3:14), keeping our eyes wide open, letting our eyes be single to the glory of God (D&C 82:19), and we'll make it just fine.

I Can Swim! Success Breeds Confidence

My daughter loves to swim. She has a natural talent for it, so when she was younger we signed her up for private swim lessons. One day she was working hard but could not master a particular stroke. Her teacher told her she could do it. I told her she could do it. We both knew she had the talent and the ability to do it, but it was when she actually succeeded in doing it that *she* believed she could do it.

We know how Heavenly Father feels about us and how He sees us. We know He knows what we can do. That knowledge can give us the confidence we need to face our life's challenges, even when we doubt our own ability to get through or past them.

Our confidence grows as we adopt God's Perspective and His faith in us. It is that confidence that spurs us to try, and when we experience success we begin to truly believe in ourselves. God may tell us we can do it, and our family or friends might also express confidence in us, but we become truly sure of ourselves when we actually succeed. Because our Heavenly Father already knows what we can do, we are not proving it to Him, but we are proving to ourselves that He is right. Our confidence in ourselves—and in Him—grows, and we are then in a position to try more, to do more, to be more valiant, more courageous, more purposeful.

I believe that is why the Lord allows us to struggle: so *we* can know what we can do and know what we can overcome. He wants us to be able to stand in the face of adversity and know who we are and act accordingly. He wants us to gain that level of confidence that comes only through experiencing success.

Go forward, giving your all, trusting in His faith in you. Experience success and claim the confidence that comes from doing what He knows you can do.

Chapter Seven

does this confidence make me look magnificent?

Experiencing the Joy of Confidence

We are more than conquerors through him that loved us.

Romans 8:37

I love musicals. One of my favorites is *The Man of La Mancha*, a poignant story of a valiant medieval knight named Don Quixote. At an inn, he meets a prostitute named Aldonza, whose life and the people in it have given her no reason to feel any self-worth. She is feisty, tough, and miserable.

But Don Quixote sees her as something different, something more. He sees beauty and virtue in her, and he tries to tell her so. He even calls her by another name—Dulcinea.

Believing him to be crazy, Aldonza resists his praises. She believes she does not deserve his devotion or his love. Still, he continues to speak to her with adoring words and songs. Little by little, Don Quixote's faith in "Dulcinea" and his love for her give her the courage to change. She dares to believe that she might deserve more than the life she has been living.

But circumstances cause her to revert to her old way of thinking and acting. Don Quixote leaves, and she searches for him, finally finding him on his deathbed. He doesn't remember her, for he was, in reality, only a deluded old man named Alonso Quijano, who thought he was a knight.

"I am Aldonza," she tells him, but he does not remember. She kneels by his bed, and in desperation she says, "You spoke to me, and everything was different. You looked at me, and you called me by another name—Dulcinea." Hopefully and elegantly, she sings to him her name, *Dulcinea*. Now, when she *acts* as Dulcinea, his faith in her and his view of her becomes her own.

Her belief in herself was planted by his belief in her, but it did not blossom until she acted in the way he saw her. Then she believed in herself. She *became* Dulcinea—a woman of strength and beauty.

The world may call us by many names, but it is the name by which our Father in Heaven calls us that is most important: *Daughter*. We are daughters of God, and we are entitled to a heavenly birthright. We have the DNA of Deity within our souls. We have been bestowed with gifts and talents that we must unlock and pursue. We have trials to overcome, burdens to bear, and adversity to overcome. We are good as we are now, but through Him we can become even better, until, someday, we will become the best we can be.

Can you see it? Can you see yourself through His eyes? Can you see the power within you? Now imagine an army of women, strong and confident, willing to believe in Him and follow Him, women who have the strength to turn off the voices of the world and the adversary and listen to Him, women who are actively and courageously doing and being their best. It is a sight that, I am sure, brings Him great joy.

We know that God wants us to have joy, but perhaps you have never thought about the joy you bring to Him. I was talking to my daughter about a good decision she had made. I smiled at her and said, "Can you see me smiling?" She said yes. Then I said, "Every time you do something good, Heavenly Father smiles, too." She was amazed at the concept that she, one little girl, had the power to make God—the Creator of a never-ending universe—smile. We all have that power.

Our joy brings Him joy. I love that idea! We can make God happy! Only heaven knows how sorry He feels as He watches His children struggle, but I know that He finds joy in our righteous choices and efforts and in our growth and triumphs. "For the Lord taketh pleasure in his people" (Psalm 149:4).

Our greatest joy in life won't come from our confidence. Confidence, though, puts us in a position to do what will bring us the greatest joy: *being an instrument in God's hands for a purpose higher than our own.* When we have the divine confidence in ourselves that comes from Perspective and success, we are more open to doing His will. Our willing hearts and obedient minds then qualify us to be His hands on earth.

The Book of Mormon missionary Ammon was a wonderful example of love and confident service. He said, "And this is the blessing which hath been bestowed upon us, that we have been made instruments in the hands of God to bring about this great work" (Alma 26:3). Alma felt the same joy: "This is my glory," he said, "that perhaps I may be an instrument in the hands of God" (Alma 29:9).

We know who we are, and He is hoping—and expecting—we will think and act accordingly. As we take His Perspective as our own and align our will with His, we will experience the joy of living a divinely purposeful life with courage and confidence.

Ask yourself: Does this confidence make me look magnificent? I know the Lord would answer with a resounding, "Yes!" It does. You *are* magnificent. You are perfectly imperfect. You are ready to light up the smallest corners of your life with your love, confidence, peace, joy, and desire to do His will. You are unique. You are needed. You are just who He needs right here, right now. You just need to realize it and embrace it.

We once were insecure and afraid, but now, because of our faith in God and in ourselves, we are confident and courageous. We have, in this way, been born again through the Atonement of Jesus Christ and the love of our Heavenly Father. "I am crucified with Christ: nevertheless I live; yet not I, but Christ liveth in me, and the life which I now live in the flesh I live by the faith of the Son of God, who loved me, and gave himself for me" (Galatians 2:20).

At the end of my life, I hope to be thoroughly used up. I hope that God sees fit to use me so often and so much that there is nothing left of me but what He has preserved, the best of me.

I want to be like Paul and say, "For I am now ready to be offered, and the time of my departure is at hand. I have fought a good fight, I have finished my course, I have kept the faith" (2 Timothy 4:6–7).

What is to be is up to me—and so it is with you. It's your choice. You know who He wants you to be. You know what you can be. Now go and do it—with confidence.

Chapter Eight

a good old-fashioned pep talk

Because We All Need One Sometimes

Even if you fall on your face, you're still moving forward.
Victor Kiam

In our eighteen years of marriage, my husband and I have learned a lot about each other. He has learned that I am emotional. I have learned that he's not psychic. A few years ago, I was really struggling with something. My husband, like most men, is a fixer. Out of love, he started coming up with all kinds of solutions to my problem. But I didn't want to be fixed. I just wanted him to listen to me.

Finally, in frustration, he said, "I don't know how to fix this, Michelle!"

I replied, "I can fix it myself. All I need you to do is listen. Then tell me that I am all right and things will be okay."

And that's just what he did. He listened to me, and then he looked me in the eyes and said, "Michelle. You are more than all right. And, yes, everything will be okay."

I felt better. That's all I wanted to hear—all I needed to hear. I didn't want advice, a lecture, solutions, or anything else. I just wanted to know I have a brain and that things would turn out fine. Even though I told him what to say, I knew that's how he truly felt. I just needed an old-fashioned pep talk.

Since then, knowing that my husband has the best intentions but still is not psychic enough to know what is in my head, I have used this same proactive approach. Whenever I am having a mini (or a large) breakdown, I simply tell my husband at the beginning of my rant, "I don't want you to fix things. I just want you to listen. I just need to hear you say that I am all right and that everything will be okay." And he does, and I always feel better. This makes things so much easier for him and so much better for me.

A few years ago I met with a dear friend who had just been through a very traumatic experience. I wanted to talk with her about it and offer some help. For two hours I listened to her and gave her a Kleenex to wipe her tears. At the end of the conversation, she noticed I was smiling. Taken aback, she asked me why.

"I'm smiling because you don't need any help at all. You are doing a lot better than you realize. Everything is going to be just fine, and so are you. You just need to see it."

She wasn't expecting me to say that. I'll be honest—neither was I. I came fully prepared to talk with her about prayer and faith and being strong and all of those things we say to try to strengthen each other. I love her and I wanted to help her, but I learned that she didn't need to be fixed or to be helped. She was actually doing quite well—she just didn't realize it.

She thought for a moment, and then she smiled back at me and said, "You know, I think you're right."

Sometimes life throws us a curveball. We make mistakes, and things are just plain hard. And sometimes we just need a good old-fashioned pep talk to get us through.

So here you go:

You are all right, and everything will be okay. ✳︎

When we feel our trials are caving in on us, it is hard to feel in control. We try to make sense of everything. We question what is happening and maybe even why. We look at our situation, which is undesirable, to say the least, and we wonder how to make it better or how it can be fixed. Will things ever be the same?

Trials are hard enough all by themselves, but we can complicate matters when we begin to question *ourselves.* We question our ability to cope and survive or even *if* we will survive. We worry that we will fail—that we will fail not only ourselves but also those who need us. We believe we are the sole pillar of strength and that if we fall, everything around us will, too. Questioning and doubting ourselves steal our ability to manage ourselves. We are our own kryptonite.

The adversary would have you believe that you are weak. He is the thief of hope and strength. He knows that when you feel powerless, you will act powerless. He wants to blind you to the fact that even when you are hurting and struggling, you can get up again.

Know this: You are doing better than you think you are. You are stronger than you realize. You will make it through.

During difficult times, it might be tempting not only to question yourself but to question God. That is, perhaps, Satan's most favorite weapon. He would have you wonder, If God loves you, why would He let this happen? He would have you doubt that God can hear you. He would have you even doubt there is a God.

But God is real. He does love you. He hears you. He will support and guide you. He has faith in you. He is the One who is ultimately in control. And as you exercise faith in Him, everything will be okay.

I know that life can be challenging. Perhaps, as you read this, you are struggling. You might be doubting yourself or your decisions.

You might be wondering if you have the strength to cope. Your faith might be wavering. Your heart might be breaking. You might be confused or tired. You might even be crying. But listen to me and believe what I say:

You are all right, and everything will be okay.

Because it's true. You can have confidence in that.

acknowledgments

I extend my deepest gratitude to those who have made this book possible:

To my dear husband, Jerey, and our children, Spencer, Paige, and Grace, who offered endless love, encouragement, patience, and support.

To the good people at Deseret Book Company: My editor, Vicki Parry, who is the light behind the prism; Jana Erickson and Lisa Roper, who offered wonderful guidance and encouragement; Heather Ward and Malina Grigg, who made the book beautiful; and Chris Schoebinger and Heidi Taylor, who saw the potential in the seed of an idea.

To my wonderful friends, Becky Smelser, Marianne Denney, Stephanie Feller, Bonnie Harris, Wendy Jones, Debbie Stoker, Laura Edvalson, Emily Kayner, Megan Anderson, Adrienne Hart, and more, who offered invaluable feedback and support.

Acknowledgments

To Angie Penrose and Kimberly Robinson, for their beautiful photographic contributions.

To the good ladies of American Night Writer's Association, Mckenna Gardner, Marsha Ward, Liz Adair, Tanya Parker Mills, Heather B. Moore, Christine Thackery, Heidi Bigelow, and many others through whom I've been exposed to amazing examples, opportunities, insights, encouragement, and friendship. Your influence has impacted me more than you will ever know.

To Lucy's parents, Matt and Stephanie Berglind, for their example of faith and eternal perspective in the face (and hands) of adversity, and for their permission to share their story.

And to my parents, S. Paul and Patricia Steed, who raised me in a home with the gospel and love and who had faith in me when I didn't have faith in myself.

And to my Heavenly Father and Jesus Christ, my Savior, in whom all things are possible.

Sources

Allen, James. *As a Man Thinketh*. Kansas City: Hallmark Cards, Inc., 1968.

Brackett, Leigh, and Lawrence Kasdan. *Star Wars Episode V: The Empire Strikes Back* [motion picture]. Twentieth-Century Fox, 1980.

Covey, Stephen R. *The 7 Habits of Highly Effective People*. New York: Simon & Schuster, 1990.

Holland, Jeffrey R. *Broken Things to Mend*. Salt Lake City: Deseret Book, 2008.

———. "Lord, I Believe." *Ensign*, May 2013, 93–95.

Kamen, Robert Mark. *The Karate Kid* [motion picture]. Columbia Pictures, 1984.

Kiam, Victor. *http://espn.go.com/espnw/quote/6391571/323/even-fall-your-face-moving-forward*.

Kimball, Spencer W. *My Beloved Sisters*. Salt Lake City: Deseret Book, 1979.

Sources

Lewis, C. S. *The Magician's Nephew.* New York: HarperCollins, 1983.

———. *Mere Christianity.* San Francisco: Simon & Schuster, 1997.

Lucado, Max. *Max on Life: Answers and Insights to Your Most Important Questions.* Nashville, Tenn.: Thomas Nelson, 2010.

Oaks, Dallin H. "Good, Better, Best." *Ensign,* November 2007, 104–5.

Old Testament: Genesis–2 Samuel (Religion 301 Student Manual). Salt Lake City: The Church of Jesus Christ of Latter-day Saints, 1980.

Schwartz, Stephen. "Through Heaven's Eyes." *The Prince of Egypt* [motion picture]. Dreamworks, 1998.

Smith, Barbara B. "A Conversation with Sister Barbara B. Smith, Relief Society General President." *Ensign,* March 1976, 6–12.

Snow, Eliza R. Address to Lehi Ward Relief Society, October 27, 1869. Lehi Ward, Alpine (Utah) Stake. In *Relief Society Minute Book,* 1868–79, Church History Library, The Church of Jesus Christ of Latter-day Saints, Salt Lake City, 26–27; cited in Julie B. Beck, "And upon the Handmaids in Those Days Will I Pour Out My Spirit." *Ensign,* May 2010, 10–12.

Tolkien, J. R. R. *The Fellowship of the Ring.* Boston: Houghton Mifflin Company, 1987.

Uchtdorf, Dieter F. "The Love of God." *Ensign,* November 2009, 21–24.

Warner, C. Terry. *Bonds That Make Us Free.* Salt Lake City: Shadow Mountain, 2001.

Wirthlin, Joseph B. "The Great Commandment." *Ensign,* November 2007, 29.

Young, Brigham. *Discourses of Brigham Young.* Compiled by John A. Widtsoe. Salt Lake City: The Church of Jesus Christ of Latter-day Saints, 1954.

index

Index

Index

about the author

MICHELLE WILSON is a stay-at-home mom, blogger, speaker, and writer. Through serving a full-time mission, teaching seminary and Sunday School classes, and speaking at firesides and conferences, Michelle has developed a love of the gospel and its simplicity. She is a lover of God, family, laughter, and chocolate (pretty much in that order). Michelle lives with her husband, Jerey, and their three children in Washington State.